HK SPORT SCIENCE MONOGRAPH SERIES

Volume 4

DATE DUE

A1   na

Demco, Inc. 38-293

Human Kinetics

loging-in-Publication Data

Athletes and the American hero dilemma / Janet C. Harris.
      p.   cm.--(HK sport science monograph series ; v. 4)
   Includes index.
   ISBN 0-87322-537-6
   1. Sports--Social aspects--United States.   2. Hero worship--United
States.   3. Sports spectators--United States--Psychology--Case
studies.   I. Title.   II. Series.
GV706.5.H366   1994
306.4'83'0973--dc20   93-29253
                                                                             CIP

ISBN: 0-87322-537-6

ISSN: 0894-4229

Copyright © 1994 by Human Kinetics Publishers, Inc.

Developmental Editors: Ann Brodsky and Mary E. Fowler; **Assistant Editors:**
Dawn Roselund and John Wentworth; **Copyeditor:** John Wentworth; **Proof-
reader:** Kirsten Kite; **Production Director:** Ernie Noa; **Typesetter & Page
Layout:** Julie Overholt; **Text Designer:** Keith Blomberg; **Mac Artist:** Tom
Janowski; **Indexer:** Theresa J. Schaefer; **Printer:** Versa Press

Printed in the United States of America   10 9 8 7 6 5 4 3 2 1

Human Kinetics
P.O. Box 5076, Champaign, IL 61825-5076
1-800-747-4457

Canada: Human Kinetics, Box 24040,
Windsor, ON N8Y 4Y9
1-800-465-7301 (in Canada only)

Europe: Human Kinetics, P.O. Box IW14,
Leeds LS16 6TR, England
0532-781708

Australia: Human Kinetics, P.O. Box 80,
Kingswood 5062, South Australia
618-374-0433

New Zealand: Human Kinetics, P.O. Box 105-231, Auckland 1
(09) 309-2259

To Larry and Mary Ann Harris

Your many years of nurturance, guidance, and love
have helped me to develop as a person and a scholar

Contents

HK Sport Science Monograph Series

The *HK Sport Science Monograph Series* is another endeavor to provide a useful communication channel for recording extensive research programs by sport scientists. Many publishers have discontinued publishing monographs because they are uneconomical. It is my hope that with the cooperation of authors, the use of electronic support systems, and the purchase of these monographs by sport scientists and libraries we can continue this series over the years.

The series will publish original research reports and reviews of literature that are sufficiently extensive not to lend themselves to reporting in available research journals. Subject matter pertinent both to the broad fields of the sport sciences and to physical education are considered appropriate for the monograph series, especially research in

- sport biomechanics,
- sport physiology,
- motor behavior (including motor control and learning, motor development, and adapted physical activity),
- sport psychology,
- sport sociology, and
- sport pedagogy.

Other titles in this series are:

- *Adolescent Growth and Motor Performances: A Longitudinal Study of Belgian Boys*
- *Biological Effects of Physical Activity*
- *Growth and Fitness of Flemish Girls: The Leuven Growth Study*
- *Kinanthropometry in Aquatic Sports: A Study of World Class Athletes*

Authors who wish to publish in the monograph series should submit two copies of the complete manuscript to the publisher. All manuscripts must conform to the current *APA Publication Manual* and be of a length between 120 and 300 double-spaced manuscript pages. The manuscript will be sent to two reviewers who will follow a review process similar to that used for scholarly journals. The decision with regard to the manuscript's acceptability will be based on its judged contribution to knowledge and on economic feasibility. Publications that are accepted, after all required revisions are made, must be submitted to the publisher on computer disk for electronic transfer to typesetting. No royalties will be paid for monographs published in this series.

Authors wishing to submit a manuscript to the monograph series or desiring further information should write to: Human Kinetics, P.O. Box 5076, Champaign, IL 61825 for further details.

Rainer Martens

Preface

I originally decided to study athletic heroes because of my interest in expressive functions of sport. It seems clear that part of the reason for the prominence of spectator sports in many societies—including American society—is that they are cultural performances (MacAloon, 1984a, 1984b; Manning, 1983) that provide opportunities for people to engage reflexively with salient societal values and social relationships. Through this process sports become meaningful to many individuals. In American society heroes are a central part of this process.

Journalistic and scholarly literature written in the last several decades is replete with suggestions that Americans no longer have heroes. But others contend that our heroes are as viable and robust as ever. This widespread debate is a manifestation of a dilemma about heroes in American society. It is tied to larger intellectual concerns about anomie, the loss of shared values. In light of the pervasive nature of this dilemma it seemed fruitful to situate my study of youths' athletic heroes in this context. I hope this book will be read by scholars, journalists, and fiction writers; one of my aims is to make them more aware of the ways that their own ideas about heroes are linked to the debate.

In chapter 1 I present and examine the debate. We learn that neither the pessimists nor the optimists have paid much attention to the opinions of the general public, which may be preventing us from moving forward in the debate. The rest of the book contributes to rectifying this oversight by examining research dealing with youths' athletic hero choices and their characterizations of the people they select. Much of the evidence consists of data from my own study of Greensboro, North Carolina, children and adolescents (data that are published here for the first time). The Greensboro data provide some of the most detailed and extensive information available concerning the people youths select as their heroes and their characterizations of these individuals.

Youths' hero choices are outlined in chapter 2. My focus is on the extent to which they select athletes as heroes, and the extent to which there are differences among hero choices of black and white youths, boys and girls, and youths at different grade levels. In chapter 3 I examine young people's characterizations of heroes, emphasizing the degree to which traditionally heroic qualities are used to describe athletes. Brief consideration is also given to differences in characterizations regarding race, gender, and grade level. In chapter 4 I synthesize the evidence bearing most centrally on the question of the continued existence of athletic heroes, acknowledge that the matter remains unresolved, and suggest further research that would shed more light on the situation.

My decision about the structure of the book did not evolve in linear fashion. Rather, it developed dialectically. I gathered and probed my own data concerning Greensboro youths' hero choices and characterizations while continuing to explore relevant journalistic/scholarly literature. The two processes fueled one another, and at times it was difficult to determine where the most important intersections lay and where the outer boundaries of the project should be drawn. Sometimes this process felt overwhelming, but fortunately there were occasional bursts of insight that led ultimately to a conceptual framework that enabled me to make sense of things. The process was not one of gradual accretion; rather, there were periods of slow progress interspersed with occasional surges of new understanding.

Several details concerning the research paradigm and the focus of the investigation need brief clarification. I chose not to locate this study in an existing theoretical model because of my desire to develop major analytical concepts from the data themselves. In the Greensboro study we purposely avoided giving respondents preconceptions about the nature of heroes. We asked the young people to think about their own heroes (the intent was to anchor what respondents had to say in concrete referents) and to voice their thoughts about what made these individuals heroic. Rather than carrying out a standard review of literature, the journalistic/scholarly literature was treated as data in their own right and analyzed discursively. As I moved back and forth between the journalistic/scholarly literature and the data gathered from young people (both from the Greensboro study and other research), several interrelated analytical concepts emerged that I subsequently used to provide a framework for the study.

Although a considerable amount of quantitative data are presented concerning youths' hero choices and characterizations, the overall paradigm of this investigation is interpretive. The goal was to understand heroes from young people's perspectives and to develop an analytical framework interrelating these perspectives with concepts developed in the discursive analysis of the journalistic/scholarly literature. The goal was *not* to ask firm, narrow, a priori research questions based on theoretical or practical problems (a scientific, positivistic approach). Quantitative data can be useful in social research following either an interpretive or positivistic paradigm.

The major focus of this work is on ideas and values, not social structure. In fact, much of the evidence presented here suggests considerable commonality among certain structural subgroups (i.e., boys/girls, blacks/whites, grade levels in school) with regard to choices and characterizations of athletic heroes. However, we should not infer from this that commonality is all there is. More fine-grained analyses should certainly be conducted to flesh out differences in the context of important structural arrangements in American society.

Janet Harris

Acknowledgments

There are always many people and organizations to thank for their help with a large research project. I first wish to thank the Research Council of the University of North Carolina at Greensboro for grants that supported my own data collection and the transcription of interview tapes. In addition, the University of North Carolina at Greensboro provided me with an Excellence Foundation Faculty Summer Fellowship and a Faculty Research Assignment. The School of Health and Human Performance and the Department of Exercise and Sport Science at the University of North Carolina at Greensboro provided support for research assistants during many phases of the work. I especially want to thank Daniel B. Watkins from the Department of Psychological Services in the Greensboro Public Schools, and the three principals of the schools in which my data were collected, for allowing me access to school-aged children and adolescents. The principals must remain unnamed to ensure anonymity of the students who took part.

I also thank the many people who assisted with various phases of data collection and analysis in the Greensboro study. Sandra L. Dixon and Maureen S. Flanigan conducted all of the interviews with the young people in the Greensboro public schools. Trudy Iddings gathered data from school records. The staff of Jackson Library at the University of North Carolina at Greensboro provided congenial assistance with locating sources. Billie Blackwell, Lorna J. Hightower, Martha J. Selby, Heather A. Setzler, and Margaret Thompson typed the interview transcriptions. Sharon L. Castleberry, Sandra L. Dixon, Jan D. Farrow, Jacqueline H. Gillis, Laura A. Hills, Betty C. Kelley, Kathleen M. Kinkema, Andreas W. Koth, Kathy M. Morocco, Ellen L. Roberts, Kimberly S. Schimmel, and Mikel K. Todd assisted with various portions of the data analysis. Sharon L. Castleberry helped with copyediting. Sylvia Eidam, Tim Barkley, and Toni B. Fields produced computer graphics. Justine J. Reel and Robert T. Clifton gave assistance with final proofing. Ann Brodsky, Kathleen M. Kinkema, Ken Scott, and an anonymous reviewer provided helpful critiques of draft versions of the manuscript. Developmental editor Mary E. Fowler was extremely helpful with the final stages of editing and publication. The assistance of all these people and organizations is happily and most gratefully acknowledged.

Chapter 1

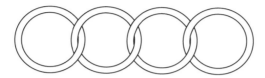

Athletes in the Context of the Hero Dilemma

Heroes provide active displays of prominent human characteristics and social relationships. Whether personal acquaintances or distant, famous figures, they are socially constructed symbols. Although definitive evidence concerning their influence is lacking, several possibilities have been examined in the scholarly and journalistic literature over the last several decades: They are thought to help define individual and collective identity, compensate for qualities perceived to be missing in individuals or society, display ideal behaviors that people strive to emulate, and provide avenues for temporary escape from the rigors of daily life.

The social construction of heroes involves interaction among people on a variety of levels. Widely famous heroes usually become known through the mass media. Television, radio, newspapers, magazines, and movies have pervasive influence on the making of these public figures. Media professionals selectively shape heroes' images, exaggerating particular characteristics and minimizing others. Media users—the public at large—also have a hand in the definition process; their perceptions and discussions about the people highlighted by the media serve to sharpen certain qualities and obscure others. Public figures themselves often take steps to ensure their own notoriety and to project particular sorts of images (Rein, Kotler, & Stoller, 1987). Heroic personal acquaintances (those known face-to-face, such as relatives, friends, teachers, and community leaders) obviously have a more limited following. Nevertheless, their images are also constructed through social interaction among the people who know them.

The term *hero* is familiar to most people. As we will see, however, it is a term that has been conceptualized in a wide variety of ways. Although it usually connotes high admiration, a person can be considered extremely praiseworthy without being labeled a hero. A number of investigators have emphasized other concepts, such as people we most admire or most choose to emulate. In the last few decades scholars and journalists have voiced frequent concerns about whether heroes even continue to exist in contemporary American society. This dilemma serves as my main organizing theme.

My work is tied to the broader topic of interpretive aspects of sport in American society. I base the investigation on the assumption that sports operate symbolically in ways similar to other popular cultural performances (MacAloon, 1984a, 1984b; Manning, 1983), such as movies, television shows, musical performances, and public political behavior. Americans interpret such phenomena in various ways, and it is their own interpretations that make them meaningful. If the meanings of such events resonate well with the interests and values of a broad range of people, then the events come to be widely remembered, familiar, and popular.

Talented athletes are clearly central components in the symbolic or expressive functioning of sport, for without them there would be no "show." My purpose here is to examine athletic heroes in American society in order to learn more about their role in the expressive functioning of sport. Those I examine include both well-known stars and lesser known personal acquaintances, but the greatest number are famous athletes.

Debate About the Continued Existence of Heroes

Perhaps the most important issue concerning the topic of heroes in contemporary American society is whether or not we still have them. This holds for athletic heroes as well as for all others. The question has been manifest in a journalistic and scholarly debate since at least the 1950s, and there is evidence that it was a topic of some interest earlier as well (Averill, 1950; Greene, 1970; Greenstein, 1969, pp. 137-143; Gurko, 1953; Klapp, 1962, p. 122; Lewis, 1965; Lowenthal, 1944/1956; Rader, 1984; Wecter, 1941). My investigation focuses on the period since the 1960s. Numerous people have pointed with pessimism to what they consider to be the deterioration of heroes. They believe that heroes no longer exist, or that those who remain are not really worthy of the title. On the other side are optimists who note changes in American heroes but do not think such changes indicate deterioration. Rather, they view them as manifestations of American vitality and flexibility.

Though this debate has remained mostly tacit or unacknowledged, the amount of attention devoted to both its pessimistic and optimistic sides warrants bringing the matter into conscious scholarly focus. In addition to failing to acknowledge the debate, the participants have brought surprisingly little hard evidence about opinions of the American public to bear in support of their positions. They start from different assumptions and therefore end up with different conclusions, but there is little resolution of the matter because their arguments are often not convincingly supported.

My analysis of athletic heroes here is placed in the context of this dilemma. Rather than initially siding with either the pessimists or the optimists, I outline the dilemma in broad terms and then examine it in more detail as it relates to athletic heroes in American society. Then I go on to address the central question of the debate—whether or not we still have athletic heroes—with research evidence concerning the views of young Americans. A considerable amount of this information consists of findings (reported here for the first time) from a 1982 study I conducted in Greensboro, North Carolina, dealing primarily with young people's choices of athletic heroes and their characterizations of the heroes they select.

Clearly optimists and pessimists disagree about whether heroes are conceived in a relativistic or an idealistic fashion. If one holds an idealistic, archetypical view, those who fall short of the ideal cannot be considered heroes. The pessimists typically take an idealist position. On the other hand, if one takes a relativistic standpoint and assumes that conceptions of heroes change over time, vary from one society to another, and even vary within a society, then it is possible to view more people as heroes, as the optimists tend to do. For the optimist, differences in the concept of what makes a hero are not necessarily considered manifestations of deterioration.

The pessimists often believe that deterioration of heroes is an indication of broader defects in modern life; they frequently tie it to their sense of widespread disillusionment in American society. Fairlie (1978) raises the common cry that our society is suffering from anomie, or loss of shared values. He argues that this loss has progressed to the point where we have a "grossly distorted individualism" in which "we are incapable of imagining the selflessly disinterested hero" (p. 43). In some cases complaints about the demise of heroes are merely convenient starting points for broader "frontal assault[s] on the shallowness of present civilization" (Rollin, 1983, p. 37).

The claim of the pessimists is that either heroes have disappeared from the scene completely or they exist in such altered states that they are no longer deserving of the label *hero* and instead should be called by another name, perhaps *celebrity*. They are known primarily for surface features such as fame, good looks, and wealth. In a frequently cited expression of our current state, Boorstin (1961/1980) suggests that contemporary "heroes" are shallow and only "notorious for their notoriety" (p. 60). They lack traditional great deeds requiring courage and passionate concern for others, such as visible and outstanding political leadership, military acumen, or moral leadership based on transcendent insights.

The pessimistic viewpoint is not a new theme. Klapp (1962, p. 122) cites more than 10 references containing this message, spanning the middle decades of the 20th century before the 1960s. Other expressions of similar ideas from the 1960s include work by Lubin (1968, pp. 306-308) and an anonymous essay in *Time* ("On the Difficulty," 1966). Laments of a similar nature in the 1970s and 1980s are pointed out by Rader (1984, pp. 185-186), who argues that the idea of the demise of heroes was expressed more frequently in these two decades than in the 1960s.

In the mid-1980s, however, several journalists and scholars suggested that our society was again devoting increased attention to heroes characterized by relatively traditional, substantive heroic profiles (Fishwick, 1983; McBee, 1985). Higher proportions of young people named heroes in a 1985 survey than in earlier polls (Bennett, 1977; McBee, 1985). The interest shown in the 1980s in

Campbell's (1968) work dealing with the notion of an archtypical hero in a universal "monomyth" is further evidence of this heightened attention to idealized, traditional heroes.

In the early 1990s we have witnessed a dizzying succession of international events, including the American victory in the Gulf War, reconfiguration of Eastern bloc economies and political systems, intense hatred and cruelty among ethnic groups in the former Yugoslavia, and civil war and starvation in Somalia. At home we are plagued with a recession and a spiraling national debt, along with other such serious domestic issues as racial tensions, drug use, abortion rights, an increasingly unaffordable health care system, and loss of confidence in elected politicians. Amid such major international and national events, it remains unclear whether American interest in heroes will grow, diminish, or stay the same. Whatever happens, the long-standing debate seems unlikely to disappear.

Once observations of the demise of heroes are made, the pessimists continue with an examination of factors thought to have been influential in bringing this about:

- American society is characterized by anomie, disillusionment, and deterioration (Boorstin, 1961/1980; Fairlie, 1978; Klapp, 1962; "On the Difficulty," 1966; Pretzinger, 1976; Rader, 1984).
- The growing popularity of television has resulted in greater exposure of flaws in heroes (Axthelm, 1979; Eskenazi, 1982; Janes, 1982; Johnson, 1983; Lewis, 1985; Meyrowitz, 1984; Miller, 1976; Pretzinger, 1976; Rader, 1984; Smelstor & Billman, 1978).
- Impulses in the general population toward an inward focus lead away from social service (Elkind, 1981; Fortino, 1984; Rollin, 1973).
- American society is characterized by heightened rationalization and technological advances (Janes, 1982; Pretzinger, 1976; Schillaci, 1978).
- There are more candidates for hero status and consequent rapid and short-lived attentiveness to them (McNulty, 1986; Rollin, 1983).
- American emphasis on equality, stemming from democratic values, makes people somewhat suspicious of widely popular, charismatic leaders (Boorstin, 1961/1980; Schlesinger, 1958/1968).

The optimists counter many of the pessimists' claims and support the idea that heroes still exist. They view American society as confident and self-directed rather than deteriorating and disillusioned. They see our increasing acceptance of diverse values and cultural traditions—including the increasing diversity of our heroes—in a positive light. Although some of the optimists acknowledge an apparent dearth of heroes in the several decades preceding the mid-1980s, they hold that Americans have not given up searching for heroes, thus implying a positive outlook on the viability of the society in the future.

To support their claim that heroes continue to exist, the optimists focus on several key points:

- Heroes vary across historical periods, across societies, and within individual societies (Browne, 1983; Cummings, 1972; Fortino, 1984; Gerzon, 1982; Gurko, 1953).
- A resurgence of interest in heroes occurred in the mid-1980s (McBee, 1985; Fishwick, 1983).
- The rapid turnover of heroes and the heightened attention to their flaws have not caused their overall demise; rather, these tendencies show that we move on to new heroes when the old ones become too flawed (Rollin, 1983).
- Fictional heroes in films and on television can still remain unflawed (Schillaci, 1978; Sirota, 1978).
- Contemporary heroes are not without depth of character, and portrayals of heroes as shallow or one-dimensional may even be a boon to hero construction (Csikszentmihalyi & Lyons, 1982; McBee, 1985).
- Even if our heroes are shallow celebrities, this may be due not to a deteriorating society but to a society in transition and seeking new directions (Klapp, 1969).
- Democracies have protections to prevent fanatic allegiance to heroes, and in itself intelligent scrutiny of heroes does not necessarily destroy their greatness (Browne, 1983; Oriard, 1982; Wecter, 1941).

It is worth noting that neither the pessimists nor the optimists have much to say about power inequities among members of dominant and subordinate groups in American society. Opposition, conflict, and struggle endemic to social relations based on such factors as gender, race, and socioeconomic status are generally thought by the pessimists to be part of the deterioration of a formerly more united, consensual society. However, the pessimists do not probe these alleged links in much detail. Similarly, the optimists celebrate American diversity, but they fail to examine the inequities and tensions inherent in such diversity and the implications of these for social injustice and the need for social change.

The charges of demise and viability have continued for many decades, partly because of a lack of definitive evidence from research. What we need is information about the extent to which the American public considers admirable people to be heroes and the ways in which heroes are characterized. Without such data, the two opposing camps continue to base their arguments on their own separate assumptions about the nature of heroes (idealistic or relativistic) and the viability of American society (disillusioned or confident). Because the arguments are based on these competing assumptions, with little evidence gathered concerning the American public's ideas about heroes, it is little wonder that movement toward resolving the dilemma has been slow.

Athletic Heroes and the American Hero Dilemma

The pessimistic and optimistic assumptions found in the general debate about the continued existence of heroes also appear in discussions focused on athletes. Three characteristics are of central importance: shallowness, flawed complexity, and compartmentalization (see Table 1.1). It is also important to note the growth of athletic antiheroes who respond to various challenges rooted in the complexities and corruptness of society. These challenges usually entail fight, flight, or resignation leading to destruction. Some observers believe that antiheroes have retained hero status, whereas others disagree. Analyses of antiheroes often touch on each of the three characteristics just mentioned.

Shallowness

The pessimists take the position that star athletes, along with entertainers such as actors and musicians, lack the traditional characteristics of heroes such as a desire to help others and the ability and tenacity to give help successfully. Instead they are deemed shallow and noted mainly for their fame, fortune, and good looks. Such a concept of the star athlete is viewed as an indication of general malaise and disillusionment in American society. The short-lived nature of athletic fame is also a problem; some think that athletes' brief periods of success disqualify them from heroism. Also, an athlete's ability is sometimes substantially trivialized. In contrast, the optimists believe that star athletes exhibit considerable depth of character and are robust, viable heroes.

Klapp (1962) points to the ways in which all heroes, including athletes, have deteriorated into celebrities whose surface qualities overshadow weak intellectual and moral standards. These celebrities maintain a front of goodness and likability that masks their lack of strong character qualities. Klapp considers this deterioration of the hero a response to societal anomie, a loss of unified direction.

Klapp (1962) stresses that Americans are especially fascinated with seeing athletes perform, putting on a good show. He believes we are more attentive to the show than to their victories. Although Klapp acknowledges that winning is still important to us, he points out that ''many American sports . . . have been

Table 1.1   Optimistic and Pessimistic Positions in the Debate

	Optimistic position	Pessimistic position
Broad assumptions	Relativistic view of heroes Society is robust and multifaceted	Idealized, traditional view of heroes Society is disillusioned and deteriorating
Characterizations of praiseworthy athletes	Robust, traditionally heroic qualities Flawed complexity is evaluated positively Compartmentalization is evaluated positively	Shallow, celebrity qualities Flawed complexity is evaluated negatively Compartmentalization is evaluated negatively

so changed . . . by grandstanding that it is hard to tell where fun in the game stops and playing to the crowd begins'' (pp. 36-37). The flashy attire of track star Florence Griffith-Joyner and entertaining end-zone dances of professional football players after they score touchdowns are recent examples. Boorstin (1961/1980) agrees with Klapp's generally pessimistic view and includes star athletes among the shallow celebrities he sees proliferating. He argues that ''their chief claim to fame is their fame itself'' (p. 60).

For Klapp (1962), celebrity characteristics are often tied to physical qualities: appearance, strength, and physical prowess (pp. 98-101). Athletic excellence depends on physical skills, and physical skills by nature have a surface quality. Klapp groups athletes with entertainers such as actors, musicians, and singers—all are noted for physical appearance and stage presence rather than deeper, more substantive virtues. Athletes and entertainers are certainly not the only well-known people who lack inner greatness, Klapp states, but he believes they are clear examples of celebrities who fail to emphasize high intellectual and moral standards, who reflect aspects of American society inconsistently, who maintain a front of likability to conceal their actual inner shortcomings, and who emphasize showmanship over skill or substance. Admirers of celebrities tend to be ''sensate people [who] move on when a surface is exhausted or when a more attractive one looms. They are like tourists—sightseeing rapidly, coming and going without deep involvement'' (p. 100).

In his article ''The Sport Hero: An Endangered Species,'' Smith (1973) echoes Klapp's (1962) lament about the demise of heroes. He comments that among sport heroes ''what we seem to have left is a collection of incomplete or tarnished quasi-heroes'' (pp. 67-68). Perhaps feeling an optimistic twinge, however, he is willing to admit that things may change in the future.

Indeed, the resurgence of American interest in heroes in the mid-1980s may have been evidence of change, but whether this will continue in the 1990s is an open question. In spite of the recent easing of international threats, there is a loss of confidence on the domestic front. Predictions are difficult concerning the sorts of athletic heroes who will emerge in our times. Our current situation might lead to an increase in the number of heroes with traditional qualities more to the pessimists' liking; it might lead to the appearance of robust, praiseworthy figures with flaws and limited appeal but who are nevertheless viewed as heroes by the optimists; or it might result in shallow celebrities without much substance who are clearly not considered heroes by anyone.

Barney and Barney (1989) hold an extremely idealized view of heroes. Although they believe celebrities and heroes both exist among athletes, they argue that celebrities predominate. They point out that ''in our worship of sport heroes we often abuse them'' (p. 13) with bribes and excessive adoration—corruptions from beyond the world of sport. Many succumb to these and do not rise to hero status; only a few survive to demonstrate heroic qualities. Athletic celebrities are noted mainly for particular athletic feats; heroes, on the other hand, are noted for long-term, consistently outstanding athletic performance, and they must also be exceptionally moral, socially responsible, and intellectual.

Athletes who engage in "off-the-field indiscretions" (p. 1) cannot legitimately be considered heroes; they remain mere celebrities. Barney and Barney believe that heroic qualities can change, that one era's heroes might not be regarded as heroic at another time. However, they also hold to their idealized, heroic archetype, suggesting that the characteristics of a hero must fall within a particular universal range of qualities.

Barney and Barney (1989), Smith (1973), and Klapp (1962) all suggest that athletes' activities beyond the contests themselves are important in determining whether or not the athletes are heroes. All four consider mere athletic excellence and other great deeds connected with sport insufficient for receiving this exalted status. In an even more extreme expression of this position, Ingham, Loy, and Swetman (1979) hold that heroes cannot arise within sport because sport is a cultural phenomenon heavily determined by more basic political and economic processes. They argue that heroes must be active leaders in the empowerment of subordinate groups, and that it is not possible to accomplish this solely within sport.

On the other hand, there are optimistic opinions on this matter. Birrell (1981) points to ways heroic character can manifest itself through actions and deeds of athletes in the heat of competition. Drawing heavily on Goffman (1967), she points out that athletic contests are risky because they are uncertain and have important consequences (e.g., money, status, career longevity) for those involved. Responses of athletes to particular situations that arise during these risky activities are likely to display crucial aspects of heroic character—courage, gameness, integrity, and composure. Birrell relativistically points out that "assessment of character focuses on characteristics highly prized in . . . [a] particular [social] setting" (p. 365). At the same time, her list of heroic character traits has an idealistic tone; she clearly points out the qualities necessary for heroism.

Agreeing with Birrell (1981) that heroes can arise within athletics, Loy and Hesketh (1984) suggest that this occurs because of an attenuated agonal system that serves as a crucible for their creation. Rooted in ancient Greece, the concept of agon refers to gaining honor by demonstrating excellence in competition. The system consists of several elements: public display of one's "personal prowess" and "moral character and social worth" (p. 43); evaluation of these by one's peers and the broader society; and public bestowal of recognition for excellence. Loy and Hesketh agree with Morford and Clark (1976) that present-day "agon motifs" are pale in comparison to earlier forms. They argue, however, that attainment of heroic status through athletic competition still occurs, and that it is tied to this special type of classic, agonistic heroism.

Ingham, Howell, and Swetman (1993) modify the earlier position of Ingham et al. (1979), leaving open the possibility that athletes may be heroic if they figure prominently in bringing about broader societal transformations. Some may simply be in the right place at the right time, while a few may take a more active role in creating social change. Relativistically, they also point out that not everyone is likely to admire the same heroes.

Perhaps our hero/ines lie wherever we situate ourselves in the political-economic issues, in whatever political space we choose to inhabit in the contemporary world in general, and the sport world in particular. (p. 204)

Another aspect of shallowness concerns the brief length of time heroes remain in the public eye (although there are no clear guidelines regarding the time span deemed necessary for hero status). Most star athletes' playing careers amount to only a few years. Coming from the pessimistic standpoint, Barney and Barney (1989) require heroes to have sustained, consistent excellence and long-lived admiration; those who do not measure up are celebrities. Taking the optimistic stance, Voigt (1978) believes that rapid turnover does not detract from heroic status. He suggests that the fleeting nature of athletic heroism may contribute to athletes' compartmentalized appeal and make them collectively more responsive to social change. It is easier to find new heroes to fit changing and splintering conceptions of what is heroic than to redefine old ones.

Birrell (1981) also takes an optimistic position on the matter of longevity and urges us to consider the deeds performed by athletes.

The names [of sport heroes] may soon be forgotten, perhaps are never known, but the substance of the achievement has served its purpose by providing one of an endless number of reaffirmations of cultural values. (p. 374)

If people tend to focus on achievements without connecting names, then it may not matter how long-lived our heroes are. Traditional depth of character may still be powerfully displayed, but in an amalgamated parade of heroes rather than in one person. Vander Velden (1986) underscores this with the speculation that heroic qualities may be more stable than the particular people who display them. From this standpoint, a large array of heroes would be beneficial because there would be a greater likelihood of full representation of the range of values and ways of behaving that are valued in our society. This line of thinking counters the notion that increasing numbers of teams and players, and frequent movement of both from one city to another, has resulted in a confusing situation that obscures heroic functioning. We will return to this shortly.

Chalip and Chalip (1989) agree with Birrell (1981) that short-lived athletic heroes may be potent forces. From their analyses of media coverage of athletes who trained for the 1984 Olympics they conclude that "the individual athletes themselves are substantially less important than are the paths to achievement which athletes generically represent" (p. 11/22). Although they believe that Olympic athletes can be powerful symbols, Chalip and Chalip are pessimistic about what Olympic heroes portray, pointing to fragmentary and shallow images. They suggest that athletic achievement is substantially trivialized by the media. Years of extensive preparation for the Olympics are downplayed or ignored completely. Olympic athletes typically come from obscurity to short-lived positions of great public attention and then return to the everyday life of an ordinary person. Fragmentary personal qualities are the main factors leading to victory. For proven champions, an obsessive personality is crucial for making them winners; for less well-known athletes, the focus is on their having the right personality to win and on potential flaws that need to be overcome. Athletes are "emptied of character" with "no ethical convictions, no political concerns, no non-sport agendas" (1989, p. 11/22).

In a similar vein, Harris and Hills (1993) show that male collegiate basketball players and their coaches are portrayed as relatively unidimensional, flat characters in journalistic accounts of the 1982 Atlantic Coast Conference tournament. Very little is said about their lives outside of basketball, and any personal characteristics mentioned are usually tied to winning. Duncan and Brummett (1987) point to the lack of depth in television portrayals of Olympic athletes, commenting on the plethora of "standardized, stock characters, caricatures who remain true to type, who are interchangeable and static" (p. 171). Numerous scholars show that the mass media tend to personalize athletic stars, but there has been little examination of whether these "up-close" portrayals are more superficial or substantive (Kinkema & Harris, 1992).

It is also frequently noted that female athletes are trivialized by the media even more than male athletes (Kinkema & Harris, 1992), and that some of this involves objectification—isolating female athletes' bodies and body parts as "things" that become the focus of attention. Morse (1983) adds that objectification of male bodies occurs as well, pointing to instant replay sequences in televised football.

Contrary to the evidence showing trivialization of athletic talent, Hilliard (1984) points out that talent is important in journalistic accounts of both male and female tennis players in the late 1970s and early 1980s. However, there is also considerable focus on personality flaws, congruent with the findings of Chalip and Chalip (1989). Females are generally portrayed as weaker because of their particular types of personality flaws. Many of the males' personality problems are seen as forgivable, but such judgments are not often made about females. Male tennis players are viewed as talented athletes who sometimes go overboard in displays of aggressiveness or temper tentrums, but such behavior is considered excusable because at heart they have good motives and they are extraordinary players. Although female tennis players are also considered talented athletes, they are depicted in the media as displaying personal weaknesses incompatible with success. These weaknesses include choking in big matches, dependency on others, depression, and failure to gain satisfaction from winning.

Chalip and Chalip (1989) contend that the trivialization of athletic achievement reduces it to proportions that almost anyone could attain. Paradoxically, however, they point out that trivialization is necessary for athletes to be heroes.

In order for Olympic heroism to be effective both as a model for achievement and as an assurance that American society abounds with persons capable of defending it from challenge, that heroism must seem within the spectator's potential grasp. . . . By trivializing the athlete's achievements—by linking success to personality—heroism becomes a matter of choice, rather than a matter of talent or luck. . . . The Olympic athlete thus becomes a reassuring representation of the American spectator's own heroic potential. (p. 11/24)

Chalip and Chalip agree with Boorstin (1961/1980) and Klapp (1962) that present-day heroes—in this case Olympic heroes—are shallow and unidimensional, with a primary focus on aspects of personality tied to athletic achievement. They clearly favor the position that athletic heroes should be judged by more than athletic competition, and that athletic excellence should not be made simplistic. Still, they contend that Olympic stars are heroes and indeed might not be elevated to hero status if their accomplishments were not depicted as within the grasp of ordinary people.

MacAloon (1987), responding to early drafts of Chalip and Chalip's (1989) work, extends their thinking by pointing out some rather troubling implications concerning American society.

Taking apart the category of ''hero'' leads to taking apart that of the ''individual'' in American cultures. How often sociologists tell us that sport enshrines and reinforces ''individual values'' quite ''natural'' in a democratic capitalist society. But what strange kind of individuality can this be when depersonalization and reduction to stereotypic roles are what we really find in most of our culture's discourses about athletes? When what we discover are not ''up close and personals'' but ''far away and impersonals''? When we see that in extreme contrast to our cultural common sense and official values, character, personality, and moral and social commitments are treated in mass discourse about athletes as radically separable? This is a contradiction that gives a sure sign of ambiguous and deeply conflicting relationships among these cultural concepts. Whatever it is that we as a people are trying to think out and tell ourselves here, it is no simple story of whole individuals seeking to achieve and unambiguously value[ing] achievement. By such a path sociologists can . . . [reach] the very center of essential social scientific questions about personhood, social relations, exploitation, and solidarity in American society. (pp. 111-112)

MacAloon (1987) pessimistically sees images of broader societal malaise centered on shallow, stereotypic, impersonal ways of relating to one another that are symptomatic of individual isolation and alienation. This is not far removed from Klapp's (1962) notion of surface relationships that exist in societal ''pseudo-integration'' (p. 111), or from Boorstin's (1961/1980) concept of the ''thicket of unreality'' (p. 3) that Americans have created for themselves.

Showing similarities to the contentions of Klapp (1962), Boorstin (1961/1980), and MacAloon (1987) that American society shows signs of frailty, Hughes and Coakley (1984) argue that lack of a well-developed self-concept may be common among members of industrialized societies. They cite data from a large national survey showing that almost half of the respondents felt they could do as well in athletics as their favorite athlete if they had the right training (Miller Brewing Company, 1983, p. 140). Hughes and Coakley maintain that this unrealistic notion is symptomatic of a weak self-concept; people with weak self-concepts often have difficulty distinguishing between themselves and others.

Goode (1978, p. 190) contends that the high level of prestige now accorded exceptional athletes has attracted more highly talented people and more technologically sophisticated training, thus widening the gap between the skill levels of elite athletes and the best of other able competitors. If both Goode (1978) and Hughes and Coakley (1984) are correct, then people are somehow able to ignore the widening skill gap and delude themselves into believing that they too could be successful elite athletes if they were properly trained.

Hughes and Coakley (1984) speculate that audiences seem more interested in relatively uncomplicated qualities of athletes, such as their playing styles and their ability to score and win, than in technical and experiential aspects of skill. They are not drawn to athletic contests to be dazzled by athletic greatness because they do not see anything especially great; almost anyone could perform as well with proper tutoring. The mass media industry recognizes this and gives audiences what they seem to find most entertaining, focusing on overall playing styles and abilities rather than on more sophisticated, technical details of play.

Leaving aside the issue of weak self-concepts, it has been noted that many who watch sport on television probably lack the technical knowledge to appreciate fully the skills of the athletes they see (Coakley, 1986, pp. 68-70). It seems likely that this lack of sophistication will lead viewers to focus on uncomplicated, shallow qualities of the players, instead of on the deeper aspects of their talents. Chalip and Chalip (1989) show that journalistic accounts of sporting events trivialize athletic talent and treat athletes in fragmentary ways. Perhaps these findings support Hughes and Coakley's (1984) contention that the mass media provide an unsophisticated public with simplistic accounts of sporting events.

Another factor influencing the trivialization of athletic talent may be the decrease in the distinctiveness of the best athletic performances. Gould (1986) shows that the mean of baseball players' yearly batting averages has remained relatively stable since 1876, although it has fluctuated over the years because of changes in technology and game rules. Over the same period, however, the variability among players' batting averages has become progressively smaller. A manifestation of this is the disappearance of the .400 season batting average. A couple of players flirted with hitting .400 in 1993, but Ted Williams was the last major league player to achieve this mark, and he did it in 1941. Gould reasons that a .400 batting average is an extreme, and as variability has decreased the extremes have been eliminated. He suggests that the general level of player performance has improved, pressing toward the outer limits:

Variation in batting averages must decrease as improving play eliminates the rough edges that great players could exploit, and as average performance moves towards the limit of human possibility and compresses great players into an ever decreasing space between average play and the unmovable right wall. (p. 63)

Gould attributes this "compression" to a larger American male population from which to select major league players, improved health of the population, and the zeal in athletics for using technology to improve performance. This performance compression phenomenon is also easy to see in races among elite skiers, runners, and swimmers, where winners and losers are now routinely separated by only hundredths of a second. The implication is "that improvement must bury in its wake the myth of ancient heroes" (p. 66). It may no longer be easy to set apart a few truly great athletes on the basis of their statistics. Other characteristics—playing styles, personality factors, or, in this era of specialization, excellence across sports—may be all that we have to distinguish the heroic athlete from the rest.

Flawed Complexity

It may seem incongruous to discuss the complexity of star athletes just after examining their shallowness. It does not seem logical for those who believe famous athletes are shallow to say these same athletes are complex. But in this case the complexity of elite performers concerns primarily the elaboration of their flaws. The pessimists hold that flaws in athletic stars are revealed by heightened media exposure. Theoretically, these flaws stem from pervasive social problems intruding into sport, leading to deterioration of heroic greatness. On the other hand, the optimists view the complexity of the athlete in a positive light—as evidence of societal variety, flexibility, and tolerance of self-criticism. They believe in the continued robustness of athletic heroes.

Nixon (1984) provides a good summary of the overall view of increasing complexity influenced by broader problems in society:

Superstar athletes with pecuniary motives, narcissistic life styles, contentious views of management, and unpopular or unconventional attitudes might represent split personalities to fans. . . . [T]he images of contemporary athletes are much more complex than the images of past sports heroes, and it can be more confusing for fans today looking for uncomplicated heroes to figure out how to react to the stars of their favorite sports. (p. 224)

Taking the pessimistic view, Rader (1984, pp. 186-195) agrees that sport has recently experienced greater incursions from the larger society. He points to an earlier period extending from the 1930s through the mid-1960s when our society seemed to be seeking national unity, and suggests that heroes helped us to do that. He compares this period to the 1970s and 1980s, times marked more by athletes who reflect "a larger cultural disillusionment" and "the invasion of sports by the realities of the outside world" (p. 186) such as player disputes with owners, player salary escalation, drug problems, and scrutiny by the media.

Others concur, pointing out that nostalgic views of idealized heroes seem to be a thing of the past (Gilbert, 1972; Kahn, 1974; Lipsyte, 1975). Lipsyte observes that in 1974 not even Hank Aaron's record-breaking 715th home run commanded adulation: "In 1974, America wasn't buying heroes, even from SportsWorld, the only hero-shop left in town" (p. 232). Rader (1984) goes on to point out that other traditional breeding grounds for heroes—politics and the military—had also withered by that time in the eyes of the public.

Hills (1992) and MacAloon (1990) examine journalistic portrayals of drug use by athletes in recent years. Hills points to a major increase in the 1980s in the number of magazine and newspaper articles dealing with drug use in sports. The coverage tends to blame individual athletes for the problem rather than looking at difficulties in sport or society at large. Athletes are characterized as having personal problems that lead to their involvement with drugs. Similarly, MacAloon examines the Canadian inquiry into steroid use by track star Ben Johnson, pointing out that he is portrayed as individually blameworthy for his mistakes.

Voigt (1978) notes a growing complexity in portrayals of baseball stars, including more attention to their imperfections. Like Rader (1984), Voigt observes "widespread cynicism toward heroes" (p. 56) in the 1970s, but he suggests the decline of the hero began much earlier than Rader claims. He contends that prior to the 1950s athletic heroes were characterized as "splendid performers who won fame through hard work, clean living, and battling obstacles" (p. 56). In the late 1950s "a demythologizing trend began to depict heroes as real people with all of the vices of mortals" (p. 56). Nevertheless, he contends that baseball heroes still exist, although they are short-lived and have specialized, limited appeal. The players insist on being themselves rather than public legends; television uncovers their flaws for the world to see—and in some cases the "flaws" themselves are part of the appeal.

> In baseball today, antiheroes like the ungovernable Alex Johnson or Joe Pepitone have enthusiastic followings similar to those portrayed by the offbeat hero of the film, *The Graduate*. (Voigt, 1976, p. 16)

The number of star athletes with the potential to become heroes has increased in the last 20 years, adding another dimension to the complexity problem. Smith (1973) points out that "there are just too many sports and too many teams for people to follow" (p. 69), and others concur (Deford, 1969; Eskenazi, 1982; Kahn, 1974; Rader, 1984, p. 194). Not only are there greater numbers of sports, but the media keep them consistently exposed to public scrutiny, creating an "information overload" (Rollin, 1983).

In addition, the 1970s advent of free agency—freedom of players to negotiate with other teams once their contracts have expired—may have muddied things even further. Some of the pessimists suggest that the illusion of player loyalty to cities and fans may have been destroyed. Free agency resulted from labor disputes between players and team owners, and the pessimists point to this as yet another example of intrusions that undermine the credibility of athletes as heroes (Eskenazi, 1982; Rader, 1984, p. 188). It is also not uncommon for whole teams to move from city to city in search of financial advantages, which might exacerbate the problem even further (Ingham, Howell, & Schilperoot, 1987; Johnson, 1985; Schimmel, 1987; Schimmel, Ingham, & Howell, 1993).

However, the cautionary notes of Birrell (1981), Chalip and Chalip (1989), Vander Velden (1986), and Voigt (1978) must be recalled. The actions of heroes may be better remembered than are the specific people who carry them out. If so, it may not matter which particular heroes are before us, or whether they command fleeting or long-term attention. Also, the pervasiveness of televised sporting events may partially counter the confusion because it allows us to continue to follow our favorites even if they leave town.

Compartmentalization

Compartmentalization of athletic heroes has to do with narrowness or limitations in their appeal. Flawed complexity may be an important factor in causing compartmentalization, as it may stem from differences in opinion over what disqualifies someone from hero status, what can be overlooked, and what is worthy of praise. Both the pessimists and the optimists agree that in the last few decades famous athletes have appealed to smaller segments of society than they once did. The pessimists, with their assumption about the idealized, universal nature of heroes, consider compartmentalization evidence of their downfall. Most mark the start of this process in the 1960s, pointing out that during that period many star athletes became identified with particular social ideologies appealing to particular groups rather than to American society as a whole. On the other hand, those on the optimistic side consider compartmentalization a sign of social vitality rooted in flexibility and openness to change. From this relativistic standpoint, heroes with strong attractiveness to particular groups are seen as signs of the malleability and robustness of American society.

Fairlie (1978), pointing to anomie and consequent disillusionment in American society, claims that we have less need for holistic heroes who can serve as common role models; we seem able to suffice with more specifically targeted people. Taking the extreme position that values are not even shared by small segments of American society but are instead different for each individual, he comments that athletes from recent decades like Joe Namath and Muhammad Ali can only be "celebrities to a number of individual and separated spectators" (p. 97). This pessimistic view suggests that most Americans live solitary and isolated lives and have no need for heroes with broad appeal who might engender a sense of shared community.

Rader (1984) does not take such an extreme position but generally agrees with Fairlie, pointing out that beginning in the 1960s highly praised athletes appealed to smaller segments of society than did their counterparts in earlier decades. He reminds us that most of the social movements of the 1960s eventually had athletic heroes associated with them, although athletes were slower than most well-known people to align themselves (p. 178). Vince Lombardi, for example, "became the hero of those troubled by the cultural unrest of the 1960s" (p. 184); Joe Namath "symbolized the rebellious youth of the 1960s" (p. 185); and Billie Jean King was broadly associated with the feminist movement, siding against "the stiff formality and pomposity of tennis in general, and . . . sex discrimination in tennis in particular" (p. 182). Pessimistically, Rader considers the compartmentalization of athletic heroes in the 1960s to mark the beginning of a decline caused by increased intrusions of societal problems into sport. In his view, the decline became more visible in the 1970s and 1980s. However, caution is advised when asserting that compartmentalization of athletic heroes began in the 1960s. For example, Voigt (1976) suggests that many baseball stars in the late 19th and early 20th centuries appealed only to specific segments of American society rather than to everyone.

On the optimistic side, Crepeau (1981, 1985) counters Fairlie's (1978) pessimistic observations concerning anomie and compartmentalization with the comment that "perhaps . . . [he] has missed part of the point" (1981, p. 29). Athletic heroes may now indeed be celebrities who appeal to compartmentalized audiences, but "this tells us as much about ourselves as ever" (1981, p. 29). Crepeau argues that heroes change as our society changes, and that this is what makes them continuously useful. Lipsky (1981) agrees, commenting that "the hero-model moves with whatever is culturally significant at a given time" (p. 117).

Crepeau (1981) also points out that fragmentation of society may not have reached the point where extreme alienation exists between individuals. Groups with shared values still seem to exist, and each of these may be attracted to different heroes who embody different characteristics. Nixon (1984) agrees that athletic heroes may appeal to particular parts of society rather than to all of it, commenting that "even if they do not meet traditional heroic criteria," athletic stars "*collectively* have the capacity to appeal to diverse segments of the American sports public" (p. 225). Crepeau illustrates by saying that longtime Dodgers first baseman Steve Garvey appealed "to those who hold what once was regarded as the traditional mainstream values," while New York Jets quarterback Joe Namath appealed "to the new urban sophisticate" (p. 29). Cummings (1972) offers similar illustrations of diverse images of three athletic heroes of the 1960s: the arrogance of Muhammad Ali, the youthful brashness of Joe Namath, and the middle-of-the-road appeal of Arnold Palmer.

Perhaps compartmentalization is tied to the short time that many athletes remain heroes, as mentioned previously in the discussion of shallowness. Differential appeal may contribute to fleeting popularity, and as we have already seen, rapid turnover facilitates changes in the characteristics of heroes in keeping with broader societal changes.

Although current star athletes seem compartmentalized in many ways, there may be particular aspects of their images that remain more widely attractive. One such aspect may be tied to consumer ideology. Nixon (1984) comments that our current athletic heroes all "sell the ideologies of the American Dream and consumption to a broad cross-section of American sports fans" (p. 225). Lipsky

(1981) uses Joe Namath to illustrate this line of thinking, contending that Namath "was able to symbolize the antiestablishment values of youth while inducing an acceptance of the larger commodity structure. He transformed the counterculture into the 'over-the-counter culture' " (p. 118). His alternative lifestyle included wearing his hair long and engaging in hedonistic sexual activity, but he also enjoyed driving fancy cars, living in a penthouse, wearing expensive clothes, and spending lavishly at New York night spots. Bloom (1988) concurs with Lipsky, commenting that images of Namath's athletic prowess constituted "a demonstration of civilized valor" (p. 70) that tended to support mainstream American values.

In spite of such similarities in appeal, the debate revolves primarily around the compartmentalized qualities of star athletes. Lipsky (1981) points out that when athletic heroes are compartmentalized some people's heroes may be others' villains (p. 26). For Americans in the 1960s, "who one rooted for began to be determined by the athlete's political views and life-style" (Lipsky, p. 117). It is clear that Billie Jean King, Muhammad Ali, and Joe Namath portrayed various sorts of alternatives to mainstream American life. It is useful to consider these alternatives in light of their potential to cause social change. In what ways might the athletes themselves, athletics, and the rest of society be altered by athletes' alternative views and actions?

Star athletes can influence social change in several ways. First, their fame and popularity may lead them to leadership roles in movements beyond athletics. For example, Muhammad Ali refused to join the army and fight in Vietnam, and he was suddenly thrust into prominence in the antiwar movement. Ingham et al. (1979) believe leadership outside of sport is absolutely essential if an athlete is to become a hero, claiming that a greatly admired athlete who does not range beyond sport to promote social change "is a pseudo-hero or celebrity" (p. 37) who serves mainly to support the status quo. Ingham et al. (1993) soften this somewhat, acknowledging the possibility of athletic heroes who are more constituted by society and less constituting of it. Nevertheless, being active in social change is an important feature of their definition of an athletic hero.

If one takes a somewhat less extreme view of the extent to which societal politics and economics determine the nature of sport, then two additional levels of involvement in social change can be envisioned, both of which are rooted in sport. First, athletes can be involved in working to transform sport by leading subordinate groups to resist dominant forces. Billie Jean King's efforts to reform women's tennis are an example. Because sport must be considered part of social life, efforts to transform sport are clearly also efforts to change social life.

Second, even when they do not take active leadership roles, athletes at times make it publicly known that they support alternative ideologies or social change movements. The mass media frequently frame athletic performances with information about players' ideological leanings, which contributes to the display of alternative ways of living. Athletes such as Ali, King, and Namath seem to have functioned in this fashion, displaying ideological positions that fall outside the mainstream.

For some, oppositional images and actions may give an athlete increased standing within the more circumscribed world of the contests; others may find such individuals distasteful. For example, white racist boxing fans likely did not celebrate Muhammad Ali's victories in the ring, and sexist tennis fans probably did not enjoy Billie Jean King's successes on the court. It is clear, however, that many considered both Ali and King heroic (see Table 2.2, page 29).

If we consider spectator sports potent cultural performances (cf. MacAloon, 1984a, 1984b; Manning, 1983) capable of encouraging public support for whatever values they display, then it is clear that athletes can help effect social change without direct leadership in movements outside athletics. It is important to remember, however, that sport and the athletes involved seem more likely to display conservative, status quo values than alternative values (Bloom, 1988; Ingham et al., 1979; Ingham et al., 1993; Kinkema & Harris, 1992; Lipsky, 1981; Oriard, 1982, pp. 51, 55; Rader, 1984, p. 178). Smith (1973) points to a number of athletes who have challenged the system and questioned prevailing social attitudes but who have not presented clear alternatives toward which to strive. Smith sees few athletes who display definite new directions for social change.

Antiheroes

There are many ways to define antiheroes, but most people would probably agree with Smith's (1973) broad notion of "someone who eschews traditional heroic qualities" (p. 67). Others (Klapp, 1962, pp. 137, 157-170; Lubin, 1968, p. 311; Rollin, 1973, p. xvii) point out that antiheroes frequently represent

- disillusionment with and alienation or withdrawal from societal problems;
- opposition to or rebellion against those problems; or
- mockery and derision of heroes themselves.

Some antiheroes are rebels with causes, while others are dropouts convinced that society and human relationships are worthless.

The topic is relevant to our discussion of the debate about the continued existence of athletic heroes because of the suggestion that antiheroes are not really heroes. Not all agree, of course. On the one hand, Smith (1973) says that rejection of mainstream characteristics of heroism by antiheroes does not affect their own heroism; they are antiheroes because they remain "heroic either in spite of or because of this" (p. 67). On the other hand, Reising (1971) suggests that athletic stars "have such a propensity for controversy . . . that they have alienated, or have come dangerously close to alienating, many of the followers of their respective sports" (p. 2). Contemporary sport literature, along with the bulk of all American literature, "mirrors an age and a society that have catapulted heroes of questionable credentials into a position of unprecedented popularity and esteem" (p. 4). Both real-life athletic stars and fictional athletes have been cast as antiheroes who "appear no more saintly than they do sinful . . . antiheroes, not heroes, are enjoying a primacy hitherto not accorded them" (p. 4).

Although real athletes as well as fictional characters can be antiheroes, the concept is used more frequently with the latter. In reference to our previous discussion of shallowness, flawed complexity, and compartmentalization, antiheroes often include athletes who

- are portrayed in shallow, trivial ways;
- are found to have serious flaws when the complexities of their lives are examined; or
- align themselves with alternatives to the societal status quo.

Nonconformist football-player-turned-movie-actor Brian Bosworth and bad-boy tennis player John McEnroe come to mind.

We have examined real-life athletes in some detail; now let's change our focus to antiheroes in sport fiction. Commenting that "anti-heroes dominate all of modern American literature," Reising (1971, p. 4) contends that fictional athletic antiheroes are not a recent phenomenon but can be found in earlier decades as well. In the early 20th century, for instance, Ring Lardner created a fictional antihero in prizefighter Midge Kelly, a bully in the ring as well as in life outside the ring. According to Reising, the evils of commercialized sport, racial bigotry, mundane social environments, loneliness, and marital discord are all grist for these fictional antiheroes.

Palmer (1973) contends that the central theme of 20th-century American and British sport novels has to do with tensions between nature and civilization. A subtheme concerns conflict between nature and intellect—body and mind. As we will soon see, one response to these tensions is to escape to a simpler, more natural life; another is to remain enmeshed in society and attempt to make changes in it; and a third is to succumb passively. Palmer stresses the third option. Athletes rooted in a simple, natural world become contaminated by the evils of big-time athletics. The tight, formal organization of spectator sport "all too often takes the natural player and changes, corrupts, or destroys him by killing the child-like and primitive spontaneity and joy that should characterize games" (p. 58). It is easy to argue that such characters have antiheroic qualities.

Drawing on the classical Greek athletic ideal of "strength and beauty in harmony" (p. 12), Higgs (1981) also emphasizes tensions between civilization and nature, commenting that the fictional athlete is "a highly symbolic hero intensely engaged in the human drama between self and nature" (p. 7). Admitting that some literary athletes are portrayed as "symbol[s] of noble aspiration toward an eternal ideal" (p. 182), he nevertheless concludes that such aspirations are often viewed as futile in many 20th-century works. Most athletes do not embark on an authentic quest for the ideal; instead they either slavishly attempt to conform to some particular societal stereotype or narcissistically worship their own bodies.

In the view of American authors, most publicly applauded representations of beauty, prowess, or versatility are suspect if not fraudulent. In twentieth-century American literature there is the unmistakable conviction that strength and beauty, the athletic ideal, must forever be sought but can never be defined or achieved. (p. 181)

The use of antiheroes in American sport fiction in part indicts stereotyped athletic heroes who conform to dominant athletic and American values, along with those who seek to regress toward youth and nature. Athletes who do neither of these but instead seek the "eternal ideal," a balance between strength and beauty, seem doomed never to reach it.

In contrast to Higgs (1981), Reising (1971), and Palmer (1973), who stress continuities throughout the 20th century, Messenger (1981) suggests that a shift in the nature of literary sport heroes has occurred in recent years. He believes that recent sport fiction contains many athletic heroes who express disillusionment with American society, especially with the athletic industry, which has become "a thriving giant of monopoly capitalism" (p. 315).

> Perplexed heroes play before disturbed witnesses in a bad time. Contemporary American fiction has treated the sports spectacle with a full range of imaginative responses that illuminate cultural dilemmas within the arena that also transcend the arena: the decline of heroism, the submission to authority, the loss of idealism, and the lack of personal validity to experience. (p. 315)

Umphlett (1975) also points to a change in athletic fictional heroes in the 20th century, comparing those of the decades since World War II with those of earlier periods. Rather than remaining in the natural world as hunters or fishermen, or continuing to struggle against the constraints of civilization, more recent heroes sometimes attempt to draw away to a private, simpler life. They ache to find a place in which freedom of expression, inwardly turned searches for personal identity, and personal achievement are possible. However, the complexities of present-day society deny fulfillment of these desires, and so the response of the heroes is to escape. No longer worried about maintaining ordinary social ties, they create an inner world of their own. These qualities are easily identifiable within the broad sweep of antiheroism.

Oriard (1982) differs from the other scholars of sport fiction discussed here in that he examines juvenile fiction as well as that aimed at adults. He argues that juvenile sport fiction "can be viewed . . . as a genre that defines exactly who the representative American hero is" (p. 25). He considers Frank Merriwell, a popular character in juvenile sport fiction in the first several decades of the 20th century, the quintessential hero. Merriwell is self-made, displays exceptionally keen prowess on the athletic field, has old-fashioned manliness, and possesses a host of other traditional qualities valued in mainstream American society: industriousness, persistence, honesty, bravery, steadiness, generosity, seriousness, fairness, modesty, commitment to duty, democratic ideals, loyalty, and willingness to self-sacrifice. Oriard contends that the juvenile heroic model "remains a frame of reference in all sports fiction" (p. 57), including that written for adults: "Since the author and reader share common knowledge of the model, the author can play his characters off against that norm without representing it in any particular figure" (p. 57). Having a common, normative hero facilitates defining other types of athletic heroes and antiheroes. A varied collection of these other types of heroes is examined by Oriard in relation to the themes found in the works that introduce these characters. The main themes include tensions between country and city (prevalent in the early 20th century), tensions between youth and age (prevalent in midcentury), tensions between men and women (most prominent in recent decades), and explorations of the mythic importance of sport (also prominent in recent decades). In common with Umphlett (1975) and Messenger (1981), Oriard sees changes in the themes expressed in sport literature throughout the 20th century (although he recognizes considerable overlap); still, he continues to call many of the main characters of these other works heroes, suggesting an underlying faith in the ongoing existence of heroes in athletic fiction.

According to Oriard (1982, pp. 51, 55), Merriwell is not only a referent for heroism in sport fiction—he is also a referent for real-life athletic heroism, and perhaps even for real-life heroism in general. Contending that juvenile sport fiction heroes in the tradition of Merriwell are still remarkably robust (pp. 26-27, 29), Oriard observes the widespread influence of this model.

In an age of disillusionment when contemporary heroes are antiheroes— embodying negative virtues of withdrawal or refusal—the athlete–hero [of juvenile sport fiction] is remarkably similar to his earliest appearances on the American scene. The apolitical, asocial, amoral, even timeless, placeless quality of the athletic contest itself enables the heroes of those contests to remain unchanged after decades. . . . Commercialism and especially tele-vision have reduced the imaginative possibilities in American sports, but heroics are still possible. . . . Every contest has its hero or heroes; sport itself is an arena for eminent heroics. (pp. 26-27)

Oriard's observation has some similarity to the suggestions by Birrell (1981) and Loy and Hesketh (1984) that real-life athletic contests are ideal locations for public demonstrations of character. As athletes perform in risky situations they display such attributes as courage, gameness, integrity, and composure. Oriard's (1982) view of the conservative nature of the Merriwell archetype also ties in well with the commonly expressed notion that real-life athletes tend to be characterized in ways that support the status quo (cf. Bloom, 1988; Ingham et al., 1979; Ingham et al., 1993; Isaacs, 1978; Kinkema & Harris, 1992; Lipsky, 1981; Rader, 1984, p. 178; Smith, 1973, 1976). In addition, the view fits with the observation that star athletes were relatively slow to align themselves with social change movements in the 1960s (Rader, 1984, p. 178).

Rader (1984, p. 178) lends historical perspective to Oriard's thinking. He suggests that real-life athletic heroes of the 1940s and 1950s consciously modeled themselves after the fictional Merriwell to serve as role models for the youth of a country in the midst of "a widespread quest for national unity" (p. 176). He believes that much of this advertent role modeling disappeared, however, with the increased prevalence of social criticism in the late 1960s. Oriard (1982) admits that "this [fictional] athlete-hero bears little resemblance to the actual heroes of the [contemporary] sports world" (p. 35), but he does not believe this traditional hero has disappeared from contemporary, real-life athletics (pp. 51, 55). Whether qualities from the juvenile sport hero persist or not, Oriard contends, he "represents one case of the American belief in the possibility of perfection. . . . [He] sustains this belief uncritically, and his image . . . continues to be potent today" (p. 55). Clearly Oriard does not think that antiheroes have completely overtaken heroes in either fictional or real-life sport.

Isaacs (1978) suggests that images of real-life football, as well as football fiction, have overlapped in three phases since the 1920s. The game and its players were first mythologized, then demythologized, and finally remythologized. We can still observe all three occurring simultaneously. Similar to Oriard's (1982) notion of a standard hero type that provides a context for numerous heroic variations, Isaacs argues that demythologization of football heroes required prior existence of a myth against which the new and different characters could be understood.

> The football hero was a fantasy that seemed peculiarly congenial to America, and we seem even now to be reluctant to let it go, preferring modifications and adjustments to anything resembling rejection. (p. 56)

The romanticized, mythical football hero had many of the qualities that Oriard describes for Frank Merriwell, but with perhaps a bit more emphasis on dramatic gallantry and military themes (cf. Isaacs, pp. 55-62). Not much football fiction existed in the early phase (mythologization), so nonfiction accounts and occasional references to the game and its players in other fiction were influential. By the late 1960s and early 1970s football fiction was more prevalent, and it was particularly at this time that demythologization altered the traditional myth; mocking and satirical antiheroes were introduced. Almost simultaneously, remythologizing tales appeared, featuring complicated heroes who present positive hope for mankind in a complex world. With these, football returned to providing fans with "a nourishing set of rituals" (p. 64). Readers sometimes encounter "a heroic version of the contemporary thinking-feeling man" (p. 65) or discover that "football is constantly giving way to considerations of the largest social, political, and philosophical issues" (p. 68). Although recognizing the existence of disillusioned and cynical antiheroes in football novels, Isaacs ends optimistically by pointing to a more recent remythologizing phase that has produced sport heroes who portray positive hope for humankind.

Webb (1974) is more pessimistic than Isaacs (1978) about football novels produced in the early 1970s. He does not see the hope observed by Isaacs, but neither does he believe that antiheroes have eliminated heroism. He points to two types of football novels—romantic and antiromantic—and says that in these stories "the myth of the athlete-hero was being tarnished but not completely destroyed by the wand of reality" (p. 454).

Renderings of athletes' off-the-field lives and behind-the-scenes workings of sport organizations graphically portray the seamier side of things in both types of novels. In romantic novels athletes' lives are simple and playful romps filled with "sex, booze, drugs, and having a good time" (p. 455), all encountered while moving forward to the glory of victory with the team. In antiromantic versions, life is more serious and complex, and anxieties about losing games and losing one's job predominate. Webb (1974) considers the latter to be "the richer vein of football fiction" (p. 456), as they examine several important issues faced by Americans: an individual's relationship to an occupation, desire for success and fear of failure, and tensions between individuals and social groups. Many would consider the characters he describes antiheroes, and some would not be willing to grant heroic status to these antiheroic fictional football greats. However, the title of Webb's paper is "Sunday Heroes: The Emergence of the Professional Football Novel," which suggests at least some optimism on his part about the continued existence of heroes in football fiction.

Summary and Preview

Whether you are a pessimist or an optimist in the debate about the ongoing existence of athletic heroes relates closely to your assumptions about the nature of a hero and the level of vitality and self-confidence present in our society. There has been no resolution of the debate partially because considerable lack of agreement continues about these two matters.

On the one hand, the pessimists favor an idealized, universal, archetypical view of heroes, maintaining that certain qualities are essential for heroism. They hold a generally negative view of American society, suggesting that anomie and cultural disillusionment are pervasive and are major causes of the deterioration of broad-based, archetypical heroes with universal appeal. On the other hand, the optimists embrace a relativistic view of heroes that suggests they differ across historical periods, from one society to another, and from one group to another within a society. They hold a positive view of American society, suggesting that anomie and cultural disillusionment are not pervasive, or that they are indications of cultural viability and openness to change rather than of unhealthy deterioration. Observations about shallowness, flawed complexity, and compartmentalization are rooted in these basic viewpoints and are important in deciding where one stands on the question about the existence of heroes.

Another barrier to resolving the debate is that arguments on both sides are somewhat lacking in rigor. Participants usually support their positions with their own observations. These observations are often well-grounded in astute social and historical analyses, but they are frequently colored by the initial pessimistic or optimistic assumptions just summarized. There has been little effort to point out evidence that opposes the favored position, and thus one is left with unconvincing, partial analyses.

In addition, there has been little use of information concerning opinions of the American public. If we can assume that the positions developed by the journalists and scholars are manifestations of those held by members of society at large, then we might expect to find similar optimists and pessimists among the American public. What is needed is direct evidence of people's athletic hero choices and their characterizations of these individuals. Such data would help us move toward resolution of the debate.

It must be recognized, of course, that American society is always changing, and these changes probably underlie fluctuations in the prominence of the debate, as well as differences in the main themes emphasized. The American hero dilemma was particularly salient in the period spanning the 1960s, 1970s, and 1980s. As we move forward in the 1990s against a backdrop of easing international tensions and increasing domestic woes, it is hard to predict what will happen. The debate may grow, wither, or remain about the same.

In the remaining chapters I want to examine the research about youths' athletic hero choices and characterizations. A major part of this research is evidence from an investigation I conducted in Greensboro, North Carolina, in 1982. My goal is to examine athletic heroes in the context of the broader American hero dilemma in order to move us closer toward resolution of the debate. It must be kept in mind, of course, that as the debate continues and changes in the future, modifications may be necessary. Heroes of young people differ from those of adults; for one thing, youths choose more athletes as heroes than adults do. If we are interested in conceptualizations of athletic heroes in American society, then it makes sense to focus on children and adolescents because of the relatively heavy emphasis they place on such individuals.

Chapter 2

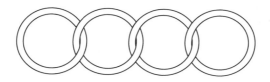

Athletes Among Youths' Hero Choices

If we know that many young people have athletic heroes, we might take this as straightforward evidence of heroes' continued existence. We saw earlier, however, that the pessimists point to shallowness, flawed complexity, and compartmentalization as signs of today's heroes' less-than-heroic stature. Information about youths' choices of heroes cannot indicate much by itself about shallowness or flawed complexity. Hero choice evidence is primarily useful for addressing the overall extent to which young people acknowledge the existence of heroes, the extent to which they include athletes among their heroes, and the extent to which athletic heroes appeal in compartmentalized fashion to particular groups. In addition, sequences of specific people chosen most frequently as heroes over a number of years indicate how long these people remain in the public eye. We can use these data to address concerns about shallowness. Later we will see that information about hero choices can give greater meaning to the evidence concerning the ways heroes are characterized.

Our examination of athletic hero choices begins with a look at the proportion of athletes among famous heroes from all walks of life; comparisons are made among athletes, entertainers, and political or military leaders. Next we compare the proportion of choices of personal acquaintances involved in sport (relatives, neighbors, friends, teachers, coaches, playground leaders, community leaders) with the proportion of choices of well-known athletes. The final section highlights differences associated with gender, race, and grade in school. Socioeconomic status (which has been shown to be extremely important in social life) will not be dealt with here because of a lack of data. This factor deserves consideration in future investigations.

Methodologically it is important to note that some people may not like to admit having heroes and may not respond truthfully to queries. On the other hand, some may be so eager to cooperate with researchers that they claim to have heroes when they really do not. Either or both of these problems can plague research on youths' hero choices, but little information is available about ways to guard against them. We can only hope that such errors have not been too great or that they have balanced each other out.

Another methodological concern has to do with the variety of questioning used in different studies. Respondents have been asked to name people who are admirable, famous, heroic, someone they would most like to emulate, and so forth. Unfortunately the body of research is small, so it is difficult to draw meaningful distinctions among different questioning approaches. Here I note distinctions between findings dealing specifically with heroes, and other evidence concerning people identified as praiseworthy but not necessarily heroic.

Each section that follows includes previously reported evidence from the 1970s, 1980s, and 1990s coupled with findings from the Greensboro study. The Greensboro data were gathered in 1982 by means of individual interviews with 128 youths from the 3rd, 6th, 9th, and 12th grades. An equal number of young people from each grade was included in the sample, along with equal numbers of males and females, and equal numbers of black and white youths. The respondents were first asked to name their heroes, and then they were asked to discuss the characteristics that made their heroes heroic. Interviewers did not give the youths a list of people to choose from, and the term "hero" was not defined for them. Our goal was to let respondents' own definitions emerge through their descriptions of the people they selected. Some went on at great length about the characteristics of their heroes, while others were more reticent. Some had many heroes, while others had few. Some discussed the praiseworthy characteristics of every hero they named, while others considered only a few. We questioned each respondent about famous people as well as personal acquaintances. We focused on athletics but structured the interview to encourage respondents to identify their entire range of heroes, not just those in sport. See Appendix A for the research methods and Appendix B for the interview schedule.

Well-Known Athletes Compared With Other Famous People

Well-known athletes are prime candidates for hero status. Information about youths' athletic hero choices can be made more meaningful by comparing it with evidence concerning well-known heroes from other walks of life. First, we can note the overall number of heroes selected. Second, we can examine ranking data of the specific people most frequently chosen. Finally, we can look at the proportions of different types of heroes selected.

Overall Number of Heroes Chosen

If we are interested in the total number of heroes that young people have, it is important to ask open-ended questions that permit them to name as many as they wish. Unfortunately, few studies have taken this approach. In many cases respondents were asked to name only one person (cf. Averill, 1950; Greenstein, 1969, p. 131; "Heroes of Young," 1980; Russell & Giurissevich, 1985; Zimmerman, 1973). Other researchers requested respondents to name several people but restricted them to choosing praiseworthy athletes (Castine & Roberts, 1974; Cooper, Livingood, & Kurz, 1981; Miller Brewing Company, 1983; Russell, 1979; Smith, 1976; Vander Velden, 1986). Some investigations permitted several choices and allowed respondents to select praiseworthy people from many walks of life, but the number of choices was limited (cf. Balswick & Ingoldsby, 1982; Csikszentmihalyi & Lyons, 1982; "Heroes of Young," 1981, 1985-1991). I have located only one study in which the number of choices was left open (Kahn, 1979). This investigation was specifically oriented toward famous heroes from all walks of life; 10 respondents named 25 people, or an average of 2.5 heroes apiece.

In studies permitting the listing of more than one praiseworthy person, respondents often identified several. Thus it can be argued that requiring respondents to select only one leads to unreliable data. If asked to repeat the task later, a respondent might offer another from among his or her complete set. In the Greensboro study the young people generally had difficulty naming just one person; they were considerably more comfortable naming several.

The main questioning in the Greensboro study involved an open-choice approach. The means, standard deviations, medians, and ranges for all the heroes named appear in Table 2.1. The figures for heroes identified in response to questioning about all walks of life (including athletics) can be compared with those named during specific questioning about athletics. Both sets of data contain famous as well as personally known heroes. The two frequencies indicate the overall numbers of heroes chosen by the sample of 128 youths. If we don't count the personal acquaintances they named, we are left with the youths' choices of well-known heroes: 477 from all walks of life (including athletics) and 382 from athletics only. As expected, there were more heroes selected in the all-walks-of-life questioning than in the questioning restricted to athletics.

It is apparent that many youths named more than one hero. They selected an average of six from all walks of life and four from athletics only. These numbers are considerably greater than the average of 2.5 choices reported in the other open-choice study (Kahn, 1979) (which might be attributed to differences

Table 2.1   Hero Selection Statistics from Athletics and All Walks of Life

	Total frequency[a]	Mean	Standard deviation	Median	Range
All walks of life	791	6.2	7.2	4.5	0-47
Athletics	510	4.0	5.0	3.0	0-39

Note. An athlete identified as a hero during questioning about heroes from all walks of life and named again as a hero during later questioning about athletics contributes to the total frequencies of both. Thus it is not appropriate to add the two total frequencies together for a grand total. Number of respondents = 128.

[a]Frequencies include famous people and personal acquaintances.

in methodology and sample). Also, the ranges and standard deviations in Table 2.1 show great variability in choices of heroes. For each set of heroes, at least one youth selected none and at least one other selected many.

If young people tend to have fairly large sets of heroes—clearly the case in the Greensboro study—then it is possible that these heroes may serve collectively to provide broad and complex images. Even if the pessimists find contemporary heroes somewhat shallow individually, the possibility of collective breadth (cf. Birrell, 1981; Vander Velden, 1986), perhaps aided by rapid turnover of relatively short-lived heroes, may mitigate an individual hero candidate's less-then-heroic stature.

Specific People Chosen Most Frequently

From the late 1970s to the present, there has been considerable interest in listing the names of famous people most frequently identified as praiseworthy or heroic by young Americans. Taken together, such lists indicate the length of time particular people remain in public prominence. This information is useful because rapid turnover of heroes is viewed by the pessimists as a manifestation of shallowness and flawed complexity; these two characteristics are seen as barriers to long-term appeal. Furthermore, in cases where the lists come from national samples, length of appeal is also useful for addressing the issue of compartmentalization. At least a few people being identified as praiseworthy or heroic over an extended period would be evidence against compartmentalization. To get a sense of longevity of the athletes compared with longevity of the others named, we will discuss the most frequently chosen athletes and situate them in the context of the most frequently chosen people from all walks of life.

Rank-order lists of praiseworthy athletes chosen most often by people between the early 1970s and mid-1980s appear in Table 2.2. One of these is based on a broad sample of children, adolescents, and adults (Smith, 1976); the others pertain to children, adolescents, and/or college students. Two of the lists are from research done in Canada (Laponce, 1986; Smith, 1976), and one contains data from the Greensboro study. Methodological and sample differences among the studies prevent us from being certain that the differences among the lists are entirely due to differences in the young people's views. Examining the two Canadian lists, we see a great disparity compared to the four generated by American youths. The Canadians emphasize ice hockey, soccer, and the Olympics, whereas the Americans focus on football, basketball, and baseball.

On the American lists, some of the most frequently named athletes are not in the most commonly represented sports. Muhammad Ali and Julius Erving are on all four lists; O.J. Simpson is on three; and Billie Jean King, Kareem Abdul-Jabbar, and Jimmy Connors are on two. Some athletes might have appeared on even more lists if data for other adjacent years had been available. This possibility is strongly suggested by the appearance of Muhammad Ali on the Canadian list generated in 1972 (Smith, 1976). We cannot tell from the available evidence what the outer limit of longevity might be. Considering all of the information about Ali, however, the limit might be as high as 11 years. Nevertheless, it is

Table 2.2 Rank Orders of the Most Frequently Selected Praiseworthy Athletes

Smith (1976)[a]	"The Top Ten" (1977)	Vander Velden (1986)[b]	"Heroes of Young" (1980)	Harris (Greensboro study)[c]	Laponce (1986)[d]
Bobby Orr	O.J. Simpson	Muhammad Ali	Eric Heiden	Tony Dorsett	Wayne Gretzky
Gordie Howe	Chris Evert	Brooks Robinson	Sugar Ray Leonard	Reggie Jackson	Bobby Orr
Nancy Greene-Raine	Joe Namath	Julius Erving	Kurt Thomas	Ralph Sampson	Babe Ruth
Karen Magnusson	Muhammad Ali	Bert Jones	Terry Bradshaw	O.J. Simpson	Mark Spitz
Bobby Hull	Nadia Comaneci	O.J. Simpson	Julius Erving	James Worthy	Pelé
Jean Belliveau	Julius Erving	Bjorn Borg	Earl Campbell	Julius Erving	Rocket Richard
Ken Dryden	Billie Jean King	Jimmy Connors	Kareem Abdul-Jabbar	Sam Perkins	Jesse Owens
Muhammad Ali	Bruce Jenner	Arthur Ashe	Muhammad Ali	Danny White	
Frank Mahovolich	Johnny Bench	John Havlicek	Willy Stargell	Muhammad Ali	
Dave Keon	Jimmy Connors	Billie Jean King	Pete Rose	Kareem Abdul-Jabbar	
Phil Esposito		Pete Maravich		John McEnroe	
Russ Jackson		Joe Namath		Babe Ruth	
Jean-Claude Killy		Johnny Unitas		Roger Staubach	
Elaine Tanner		Chris Evert			
Babe Ruth					
Pelé					
Wilt Chamberlain					
Rusty Staub					

[a]Canadian study; data gathered in 1972; sample includes children, adolescents, and adults; [b]Data gathered in 1978; [c]Data gathered in 1982; includes athletes considered either admirable or heroic; [d]Canadian study.

Table 2.3   Rank Orders of the Most Frequently Selected Praiseworthy People From All Walks of Life

"Heroes of Young" (1980)	"Heroes of Young" (1981)	Harris (Greensboro study)[a]	"Heroes of Young" (1985)	"Heroes of Young" (1986)
Burt Reynolds	Burt Reynolds	Ronald Reagan	Eddie Murphy	Bill Cosby
Steve Martin	Richard Pryor	Martin Luther	Ronald Reagan	Sylvester
Eric Heiden	Alan Alda	King, Jr.	Bill Cosby	Stallone
Erik Estrada	Brooke Shields	Tony Dorsett	Prince	Eddie Murphy
Alan Alda	John Ritter	Burt Reynolds	Sylvester	Ronald Reagan
Kristy	Scott Baio	George	Stallone	Chuck Norris
McNichol	Bo Derek	Washington	Clint Eastwood	Clint Eastwood
Sugar Ray	George Burns	Diana Ross	Debbie Allen	Molly
Leonard	Sugar Ray	Reggie Jackson	Michael Jordan	Ringwald
Scott Baio	Leonard	Superman	Madonna	Rob Lowe
John Belushi	Steve Martin	Bugs Bunny	Mary Lou	Arnold
Robin Williams		Ralph	Retton	Schwarzenegger
		Sampson	Bruce	Don Johnson
			Springsteen	Michael J. Fox
			Eddie Van Halen	
			Harrison Ford	

(continued)

clear that a rapid turnover of highly admired athletes occurred during this period. Most people appeared on only one list.

Similar rank-order lists of the most frequently selected praiseworthy people from all walks of life are also available. Most of these were obtained from national samples of secondary school students in annual polls throughout the 1980s and early 1990s ("Heroes of Young," 1980, 1981, 1985-1991). Although the questions varied somewhat from year to year, respondents were usually asked to name the person(s) in public life they admired the most. Their top choices appear in Table 2.3, along with a similar list from the Greensboro study. Michael Jordan is on six of the lists; Eddie Murphy and Bill Cosby show up on five; Ronald Reagan and Tom Cruise appear on four; and Clint Eastwood, Oprah Winfrey, Burt Reynolds, Sylvester Stallone, and Arnold Schwarzenegger are on three. Only one athlete—Michael Jordan—appears among those with longevity of 3 years or more, and he tops everyone with 6 years.

Although he has retired from professional basketball, Michael Jordan will likely continue his string of years in the future, which will raise the outer limit even higher. His popularity might be blunted for some by media attention to such things as his alleged connections to gamblers and instances of his fighting

Table 2.3   *(continued)*

"Heroes of Young" (1987)	"Heroes of Young" (1988)	"Heroes of Young" (1989)	"Heroes of Young" (1990)	"Heroes of Young" (1991)
Tom Cruise	Eddie Murphy	Michael Jordan	Paula Abdul	H. Norman
Bill Cosby	Michael Jordan	Ronald Reagan	Mother	Schwarzkopf
Michael Jordan	Bill Cosby	Donald Trump	Michael Jordan	Julia Roberts
Eddie Murphy	Oprah Winfrey	Tom Cruise	Father	George Bush
Kirk Cameron	Patrick Swayze	Eddie Murphy	Barbara Bush	Michael Jordan
Bruce Willis	Arnold	Bill Cosby	Oprah Winfrey	Barbara Bush
Michael J. Fox	Schwarzenegger	Mikhail	Nelson Mandela	Mariah Carey
Mother Theresa	Oliver North	Gorbachev	Donald Trump	Kevin Costner
Mel Gibson	Mike Tyson	Jesse Jackson	George Bush	Oprah Winfrey
Arnold	Jesse Jackson	Magic Johnson	Tom Cruise	Madonna
Schwarzenegger	Larry Bird	Patrick Swayze	Janet Jackson	Paula Abdul
Clint Eastwood	Tom Cruise			Sandra Day
	Whitney			O'Connor
	Houston			
	Sylvester			
	Stallone			

[a]Data gathered in 1982; includes praiseworthy people considered either admirable or heroic.

in a game, but his continuing success in commercial advertising seems likely to ensure his fame for quite some time to come. Leaving Jordan aside, brief appearances of 1 or 2 years were most common, which indicates quite rapid turnover. Except for the list from the Greensboro study, the lists are all based on similar methodology and sampling. We can therefore rule out methodological dissimilarities as a possible explanation for the difference. The likelihood seems strong that the rapid turnover is due to changes in youths' ideas about who is praiseworthy.

We will see that athletes, entertainers, and political and military leaders are the most frequently selected types of famous heroes. Let's look briefly at the praiseworthy people chosen most often in each of these categories in the Greensboro study (see Tables 2.4, 2.5, and 2.6). The people at the top of each of these groups make up the Greensboro list in Table 2.3 (three athletes, four entertainers, and three politicians or military leaders). Ronald Reagan was chosen by 30 of the Greensboro youths, the most frequently selected person in the investigation. Martin Luther King, Jr., was a close second with 27. The rest were chosen considerably less often. This is of interest because there were 128 respondents; even the most popular person was chosen only by about one fourth of the sample. These results suggest compartmentalization; there was little agreement among selections.

Table 2.4   Top Athletes Selected[a]

Name	Number of respondents who selected the person
Tony Dorsett	17
Reggie Jackson	15
Ralph Sampson	12
O.J. Simpson	9
James Worthy	9
Julius Erving	7
Sam Perkins	6
Danny White	5
Muhammad Ali	4
Kareem Abdul-Jabbar	4
John McEnroe	4
Joe Montana	4
Babe Ruth	4
Roger Staubach	4

Note. Total number of different athletes selected = 96. Total number of respondents' selections (counting the same athlete more than once if selected by more than one respondent) = 214.

[a]Includes athletes considered admirable and/or heroic. Data are from general section of the interview. A single respondent's choice of a particular athlete as *both* admirable and heroic is counted only once.

If we agree with the pessimists that longevity is important for hero status, then we need to know, "How long is long enough?" There is no easy answer. The pessimists do not provide guidelines, and no comparisons can be made with earlier decades in the 20th century because similar series of lists for these periods have not been found. No matter what length of time is thought sufficient, it is also important to know how many people must achieve this standard before the pessimists will be willing to acknowledge that American heroes have not disappeared. There are no guidelines for this, either. Without such evaluative criteria we can only acknowledge the outer limits and the more common durations of high public visibility. Similarly, there are no evaluative criteria against which to judge evidence of compartmentalization. Does selection by only one fourth of the sample represent compartmentalization, or not? We don't know.

Compartmentalization and lack of criteria to determine longevity are just two examples of the general problem I mentioned earlier: Criteria against which to judge evidence in relation to the debate about the ongoing existence of athletic heroes are lacking. Just how strong does evidence have to be to suggest that our heroes have died off or if the opposite is true? I have tried to answer this question based on careful weighing of relevant information. The possibility that the information might not be sufficient should be kept in mind as our discussion progresses.

Table 2.5   Top Entertainers Selected[a]

Name	Number of respondents who selected the person
Burt Reynolds	17
Diana Ross	16
Superman (Christopher Reeve)	13
Bugs Bunny	12
Wonder Woman (Lynda Carter)	10
Brooke Shields	9
Magnum, P.I. (Tom Selleck)	8
Elvis Presley	8
Stevie Wonder	8
Carol Burnett	7
Michael Jackson	7

Note. Total number of different entertainers selected = 234. Total number of respondents' selections (counting the same entertainer more than once if selected by more than one respondent) = 462.

[a]Includes entertainers considered admirable and/or heroic. Data are from general section of the interview. A single respondent's choice of a particular entertainer as *both* admirable and heroic is counted only once.

Proportions of Different Types of Heroes Chosen

Clearly, athletes, entertainers, and political leaders are the three kinds of famous heroes selected most often. Selections of people identified as praiseworthy but not necessarily heroic follow a similar pattern. Very small numbers of others were chosen, such as religious leaders, military leaders, explorers, scholars, inventors, humanitarians, and literary figures. In data gathered since the late 1940s, between one third and well over one half of the famous people selected have been athletes and entertainers (Averill, 1950; Balswick & Ingoldsby, 1982; Greenstein, 1969, p. 138; Kahn, 1979; Russell & Giurissevich, 1985; Zimmerman, 1973). Politicians have comprised one fourth or less of the choices (Balswick & Ingoldsby, 1982; Greenstein, 1969; Kahn, 1979; Zimmerman, 1973).

We saw earlier that athletes and entertainers comprise a large proportion of the most frequently mentioned people both in several large polls of American secondary school students ("Heroes of Young," 1980, 1981, 1985-1991) and in the Greensboro study (see Table 2.3). Looking collectively at these, it can be seen that people with 3 to 6 years longevity on the lists include eight entertainers, one athlete, and one politician.

However, findings from two studies are incongruent with these results. In an investigation of a combined sample of adolescents and adults, about one third said they would prefer to be an athlete or a movie star, just over one third chose to be

Table 2.6   Top Political or Military Leaders Selected[a]

Name	Number of respondents who selected the person
Ronald Reagan	30
Martin Luther King, Jr.	27
George Washington	17
Abraham Lincoln	10
Jimmy Carter	8
John F. Kennedy	6
George Patton	5
George Bush	4
Theodore Roosevelt	4
Queen Elizabeth	3
James Hunt (North Carolina governor)	3
Douglas MacArthur	3
Franklin D. Roosevelt	3

Note. Total number of different political or military leaders selected = 41. Total number of respondents' selections (counting the same political or military leader more than once if selected by more than one respondent) = 159.

[a]Includes political or military leaders considered admirable and/or heroic. Data are from general section of the interview. A single respondent's choice of a particular political or military leader as *both* admirable and heroic is counted only once.

a famous scientist, and about one seventh preferred to be a famous statesperson (Miller Brewing Company, 1983). This is the only investigation in which scientists were chosen by a substantial proportion of the respondents. Finally, in a poll of college students, the praiseworthy public figures most often selected include 45% athletes and entertainers, 18% politicians, and 36% others—religious and humanitarian figures, explorers, scientists ("Among Wisconsin Students," 1985). There are no ready theoretical explanations for these divergent results, except to note that two of these studies included college students and adults rather than children and adolescents. It is clear that adults select fewer athletes and entertainers (Castine & Roberts, 1974; Hyman, 1975; Mueller, 1973; Smith, 1986).

Considering athletes and entertainers specifically, the relative proportions selected by respondents have varied, but entertainers tend to predominate. In 12 studies, more entertainers than athletes are named by college students ("Among Wisconsin Students," 1985) and young people (Balswick & Ingoldsby, 1982; "Heroes of Young," 1980, 1981, 1985-1991; Russell & Giurissevich, 1985). In three investigations, athletes are selected more frequently; one sample includes adults and teenagers (Miller Brewing Company, 1983), and two consist solely of young people (Kahn, 1979; Zimmerman, 1973).

In the Greensboro study the respondents were asked in one part of the interview to name famous heroes in general, including athletes and all others (see Appendix A and Appendix B). The people they named were categorized into four walks of life: athletics, entertainment, politics or the military, and other (e.g., religion, science, exploration, health). Most of their heroes were associated with the first three categories, and most people in these categories were famous athletes, entertainers, and political or military leaders. A handful of individuals in these three walks of life were involved in other ways (e.g., in sport—coaches, sportscasters; in entertainment—models, authors; in politics or the military—staff members to politicians). Because most of the people were athletes, entertainers, and political or military leaders, however, these terms are used here to refer comprehensively to each of these sets of heroes.

Entertainers constituted about one half of the Greensboro youths' famous heroes, athletes comprised about one fourth, and political and military leaders accounted for about one fifth of the total (see Figure 2.1). The percentages on the diagram in Figure 2.1 and the others like it total to 100%, with a few minor discrepancies due to rounding errors. Famous athletes clearly constituted an important segment of these youths' well-known heroes, but it is important to keep in mind that about three fourths of them were *not* involved centrally in athletics. At the same time, athletes and entertainers together constituted about three fourths of the total.

Returning to the debate, it is clear that limited proportions of athletes routinely get chosen as heroes. Once again, this direct evidence of selection suggests

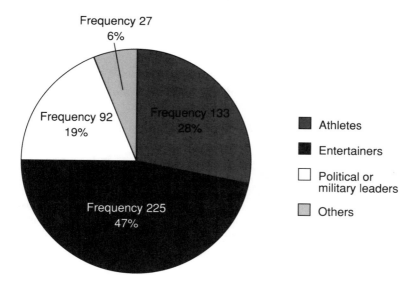

Figure 2.1.   Walks of life of youths' famous heroes. Data are from the general section of the interview. Number of respondents = 128.

that athletic heroes still exist. As we know, however, evidence about hero choices is not very useful by itself for resolving questions about shallowness. The heavy preponderance of athletes and entertainers in youths' hero choices leaves open the possibility that the pessimists are right about the overall demise of heroes. They point to both as prime examples of shallow celebrities who lack traditionally heroic breadth and depth. To be more definitive we need to know the extent to which and the ways in which shallowness influences young people's characterizations of their heroes, and we need to compare athletic heroes with those from other walks of life.

Summary and Implications: Well-Known Athletes Compared With Other Famous Heroes

We know that athletes are selected as heroes by young people, which suggests these heroes still exist. Athletes also appear occasionally on lists of most frequently selected heroes. Most of them have rather limited longevity on such lists, however, and this leaves open the possibility of shallowness, flawed complexity, and compartmentalization. However, Michael Jordan is the current record-holder among all types of heroes, with a longevity of 6 years. But most athletic heroes are not selected by very large proportions of respondents, which suggests they may have limited or compartmentalized appeal. Finally, athletic heroes constitute a limited proportion of the total number of famous heroes that young people select—probably about 25%. If athletes turn out to be particularly reprehensible as heroes, perhaps the situation would not be as dire as it might first appear because other types of heroes in greater numbers might compensate. This, coupled with the fact that most youths select several heroes, leaves open the possibility that all of them may collectively display a considerable amount of traditional heroism.

Athletic Personal Acquaintances Compared With Well-Known Athletes

It is important to examine the extent to which young people include personal acquaintances among their athletic heroes. Most of the people perceived by youths to be influential in their lives are personal acquaintances. In a study of teenagers it was found that 97% of the people identified as most influential were known personally (McCormack, 1984).

Also, some think that personal acquaintances have the potential to be conceptualized in more substantive, traditionally heroic ways. For example, Klapp (1962) adds a comparative observation about personal acquaintances to his depiction of the shallowness of celebrities. Characteristics of people we know personally usually undergo minimal abstraction and elaboration because we have "neither the freedom nor need to build a legend" (p. 13). Klapp goes on to differentiate further between the two.

> The image [of a personal acquaintance] is likely to be more concrete—less typical—because [it is] not abstracted through the interaction of thousands.

It is a more complete personality because people know several "sides" of the person. . . . Fewer people are using him and he is less perfected as a daydream image. Yet the difference between the typing of ordinary persons and that of celebrities is of degree rather than kind—the degree of abstraction, elaboration, and truth. (pp. 13-14)

From this perspective, if heroes exist at all they might turn out to be personal acquaintances, people who are perceived to have more complete personalities, more depth of character. However, Klapp questions whether even personal acquaintances have the requisite depth and wholeness to be heroes, observing that shallowness of public figures is an indication of widespread shallowness in social relationships in American society in general—including face-to-face relationships. Furthermore, our more intimate knowledge of personal acquaintances may lead us to see serious flaws that preclude them from becoming heroes.

Several types of information are useful for examining personally known athletic heroes in relation to famous ones. First, we can note the extent to which famous athletes are personalized by their admirers and the media. Second, we can look at the relative proportions of personal acquaintances and public figures among athletic heroes. Finally, we can observe the relative proportions of admirers who decline to identify personal acquaintances and/or public figures as athletic heroes.

Personalization of Famous Athletes

If personally known athletes have the potential to be more traditionally heroic, then to the extent that people personalize famous athletes these more distant figures might have similar possibilities. Although the available evidence is indirect and limited, it seems both to support and oppose personalization. A central issue is the extent of loyalty and close ties felt by the general public toward players and teams.

We turn first to the oppositional findings. In interviews with metropolitan residents—primarily adults—Anderson (1979) found that more people have favorite teams than favorite players. Free agency makes professional player movements from team to team quite common, and thus it might be easier to admire a team rather than individual players; teams move occasionally, but not as frequently as athletes. Players also come and go as they move from high school, to college, to the professional ranks, and eventually to retirement. Pretzinger (1976) and Schillaci (1978) point out that our technologically and organizationally complex world may partially submerge individuals, making it easier to applaud group efforts. Admiration of teams over players suggests that people keep players at a distance rather than personalizing them.

In a related vein, Skipper (1984, 1985) points to a decline in nicknames for major league baseball players since the 1920s, and especially since the 1950s. He assumes that nicknames indicate close personal identification and suggests that their decline marks a deterioration of the "folk hero" status of baseball players. He ties this deterioration to commercialization and to the heavy emphasis on money in sport, suggesting that players now seem less loyal to fans.

However, nicknames have not completely disappeared from professional athletics—as evidenced by "Doctor J," "Hakeem the Dream," and "Magic Johnson"—which may indicate that close identification with players is not completely dead. There is also evidence of ongoing loyalty. In a survey of sports fans (including many adults), Kennedy and Williamson (1978) inquired about allegiance to star players and favorite teams. They found that respondents were not alienated to any great extent by athletes making more money and switching teams more. Overall, fans believe their interest in sport, fun in watching games, loyalty to favorite teams, and enthusiasm for star players all increased in the 5 years prior to the study. In addition, over half of the respondents agree that professional athletes are good examples for young people, while only about a third believe they are not. In a later study of adults and young people, 75% of the respondents thought athletes are good role models for children, while 59% thought they are the best role models children can have (Miller Brewing Company, 1983).

If a continuing loyalty to individual athletes persists, it might be partly because the mass media tend to portray them in "up close and personal" ways. We saw earlier, however, that media portrayals at times trivialize athletic talent, fragment personalities, and dwell on personal flaws (cf. Chalip & Chalip, 1989; Duncan & Brummett, 1987; Harris & Hills, 1993; Hilliard, 1984; Hills, 1992; Kinkema & Harris, 1992; MacAloon, 1990).

This information about fan loyalty offers only limited insights about personalization of famous athletes and so is of limited usefulness in terms of addressing the debate. Furthermore, what little evidence exists is equivocal in that it shows both loyalty to individual athletes and the lack of it. Finally, even if we assume that personalization occurs, we cannot tell from the evidence whether it is tied to people's characterizations of famous athletes. We learn nothing about whether personalization results in the subversion of shallowness and enhancement of traditionally heroic qualities, or whether it tends to magnify flawed complexity.

Proportions of Personal Acquaintances and Well-Known People Chosen as Athletic Heroes

If personal acquaintances involved in athletics turn out to be more traditionally heroic than famous athletes, then it is important to know the relative proportions of the two among people's athletic heroes. Large proportions of personal acquaintances might tend to dilute the shallowness and flawed complexity of the public figures.

The evidence comes primarily from the Greensboro study (see Appendix A and Appendix B). Personally known individuals chosen as athletic heroes included relatives, neighbors, friends, teachers, coaches, playground leaders, and community leaders. Most were active players, but some were coaches, and a few others took part in such activities as cheerleading or weight room workouts. Most played team sports, but a few participated in individual or dual sports.

First, it should be noted that when the Greensboro youths were asked to name their full set of heroes from all walks of life—public figures along with personal acquaintances—very few of the people identified were personal acquaintances involved in athletics. Famous athletes comprised 17% of the total, while personal acquaintances involved in athletics amounted to only 8%. Personal acquaintances thus comprised about one third of the complete number of athletic heroes named here. Furthermore, in most cases the athletic ties of personal acquaintances were mentioned in rather matter-of-fact ways without any particular emphasis on their praiseworthiness. Personal acquaintances involved in athletics were held in high esteem quite often for qualities associated with areas of life other than athletics.

In questioning specifically about athletic heroes, the Greensboro youths identified 382 famous athletes (75% of the total) and 128 athletic personal acquaintances (25% of the total). In another study focused specifically on athletes, the choices of children and adolescents were reported to be 88% public figures and 12% personal acquaintances (Cooper et al., 1981). All of these findings together suggest that personal acquaintances comprise between one tenth and one third of young people's athletic heroes.

If athletic personal acquaintances are not particularly prominent among youths' heroes, then the possibility that they have more robust and more traditionally heroic characteristics than famous athletes may be a moot point in terms of the debate. Nevertheless, we saw earlier that young people generally think personal acquaintances are much more likely to be influential in their lives. This suggests that personally known athletic heroes should not be dismissed merely because of their small numbers.

Declining to Name Personal Acquaintances and Well-Known People as Athletic Heroes

When youths are asked to name athletes they hold in high regard, some say there are none. Along with information about the number of highly praised athletes people name, knowledge of the proportion who decline to name anyone provides direct evidence concerning the debate. The unwillingness of large proportions of young people to identify athletic heroes would call their existence into question. It seems likely that such respondents either do not pay much attention to athletics or do not consider athletes heroic.

In most studies where information of this sort is reported the focus is on "favorite athletes" or "admirable athletes" rather than on heroes. This is problematic because we cannot be sure that respondents who decline to name favorite or admirable athletes would also decline to name heroes (although any athlete called heroic would also likely be labeled admirable). Data from the Greensboro study pertain specifically to heroes.

It is often difficult for respondents (especially young people) to disobey researchers' requests for information. When they agree to participate they often tacitly commit themselves to cooperating as fully as possible. On the other hand, some people may not want to admit they have heroes. In light of these two opposite possibilities it seems important for researchers to try to legitimate either answer. But because descriptions of such attempts are usually not included in research reports, it is hard to know how much faith to place in information about proportions of people who decline to identify an athletic hero.

In the Greensboro study, questions about the youths' hero choices were preceded by comments from the interviewer aimed at making it legitimate for respondents to say that they had no heroes (see Appendix A and Appendix B). If evidence from the Greensboro study or other investigations is in error, however, it probably errs toward underrepresenting the number of youths who actually had no heroes. In the Greensboro study most of the young people were very eager to respond, so an interviewer's efforts to legitimize a negative response might not have been effective.

Vander Velden (1986) reports that in 1978 only 15% of a sample of college students chose to call the famous athletes they looked up to "heroes," while 58% tagged them as "favorite players." Cooper et al. (1981) show that 15% of a sample of children and adolescents did not identify a sport hero. In a national sample of teenagers, 15% of the boys and 32% of the girls said they did not admire any athletes (Decision Research Corporation, 1984). Bredemeier, Weiss, Shields, and Cooper (1986) also report that among children in grades 4 through 7, 37% of the boys and 57% of the girls did not answer a question asking them to name a favorite athlete. Among a broad-based sample (including youths and adults) in the Canadian city of Edmonton, somewhat over half of the respondents said there was no athlete they would like to be like (Smith, 1976). This high percentage in the Canadian study may be due to the relatively large number of adults in the sample. As a passing note, it is also interesting that two studies show considerably more girls declining to name highly esteemed athletes than boys (Bredemeier et al., 1986; Decision Research Corporation, 1984).

Vander Velden (1986) and Cooper et al. (1981) report the only evidence beyond the Greensboro study pertaining specifically to heroes. Compared to their findings, the Greensboro youths fell in the middle, with 24% declining to name famous, well-known athletes as heroes and 48% declining to identify heroes among personally known athletes. Hero status was clearly more doubtful for personally known athletes, which is congruent with the smaller proportion of personal acquaintances among the total number of athletes chosen as heroes noted previously. Overall, 18% of the children and adolescents in the Greensboro study named no athletic heroes at all, neither well-known athletes nor personal acquaintances. Differences between the results obtained by Vander Velden, Cooper et al., and the Greensboro study may be due to sampling and methodological dissimilarities.

In terms of the debate, it is clear that not all youths turn away from identifying athletes as heroes. Many respondents name several, while others choose none. Those who choose none would probably agree that athletic heroes do not exist, while those who select them would probably say they do exist. As we saw earlier, however, to move closer toward resolving the argument we need information about the ways in which respondents characterize athletic heroes in terms of traditional heroism versus shallowness, flawed complexity, and compartmentalization.

Summary and Implications: Heroic Personal Acquaintances Involved in Athletics Compared With Heroic Well-Known Athletes

Personal acquaintances who are praiseworthy athletes seem less prominent than highly commendable, famous athletes. Fewer of them are selected, and young people more often refuse to identify them as heroes. Furthermore, there is only tangential and limited evidence suggesting that famous athletes are personalized by their admirers and the mass media. Personal, face-to-face knowledge of athletic heroes is in somewhat short supply. Care must be taken in generalizing from these findings because they come almost exclusively from the Greensboro study. If personal acquaintances chosen as heroes are more robust and traditionally heroic than public figures, then the large number of famous athletic heroes chosen may point toward their shallowness and flawed complexity. Of course we need evidence of athletic hero characterizations to address this adequately. Also, even a handful of personally known athletic heroes may be important because personal acquaintances are more often perceived as influential in young people's lives.

Gender, Race, and Grade Comparisons

American society contains a myriad of distinct and yet crisscrossing social formations associated with a wide range of life experiences, values, and possibilities for self-determination. Amidst this enormous variety, considerable diversity in people's hero choices is likely. If athletic heroes are chosen often by particular groups and seldom by others, this would suggest compartmentalized appeal. Still more fine-grained compartmentalization would be implied if particular groups selected different types of athletic heroes more frequently. One way of addressing such possibilities is to compare youths' hero choices in terms of gender, race, and grade in school. Many of the kinds of evidence used previously are employed here to point out differences centered on these three factors.

Gender Comparisons

Though more women are involved in sport every year, it is still true that there are fewer females than males among famous athletes in American society. Hence it is not surprising to find that famous players chosen as praiseworthy have more often been males. When asked to name the male and female athlete they most identify with, female high school athletes named a wide variety of males and a much smaller set of females (Marovelli & Crawford, 1987). Women and girls vary between selecting almost entirely male athletes and choosing substantial numbers of female players along with the male players. Men and boys, on the other hand, consistently select almost entirely male athletes. Most studies show that males predominate in people's choices of highly esteemed athletes (Balswick & Ingoldsby, 1982; Bredemeier et al., 1986; Cooper et al., 1981; "Heroes of Young,'' 1980; Laponce, 1986; Miller Brewing Company, 1983; Smith, 1976; ''The Top Ten,'' 1977; Vander Velden, 1986). Running counter to this, however, are two studies showing that women and girls named relatively large numbers of female athletic heroes (Smith, 1976; Bredemeier et al., 1986).

In line with most findings, it was found in the Greensboro study that both boys and girls selected high proportions of males among famous athletic heroes. When asked to name famous athletic heroes, boys chose 100% males and girls chose 82% males (see Figure 2.2). In response to broader questions about famous heroes from all walks of life, the athletes identified consisted of 100% males for the boys (their few famous female heroes were all entertainers), and 67% males for the girls (see Figures 2.3 and 2.4).

Athletic heroes were not the most heavily male, however. As might be expected, male heroes were even more common among political or military leaders—primarily because the girls chose fewer females in this category whereas the boys chose 100% males (see Figure 2.4). Comparing athletes, entertainers, and political or military leaders, entertainers were the most heavily female. Among entertainers, females comprised 11% of the boys' choices and 37% of the girls'. This focus on female entertainers is also supported by findings from national samples of secondary school students in the 1980s and early 1990s; the small number of famous females chosen by respondents consisted of 13 entertainers, 1 athlete, and 2 political or military leaders (see Table 2.3) (''Heroes of Young,'' 1980, 1981, 1985-1991).

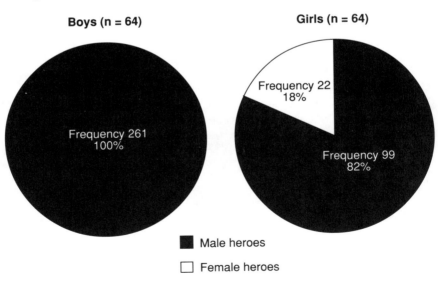

Figure 2.2.   **Gender of boys' and girls' famous athletic heroes from sport-only questioning.** Note the difference in the total frequency of heroes represented on each chart. Overall frequency = 382.

Boys (n = 64)   **Girls (n = 64)**

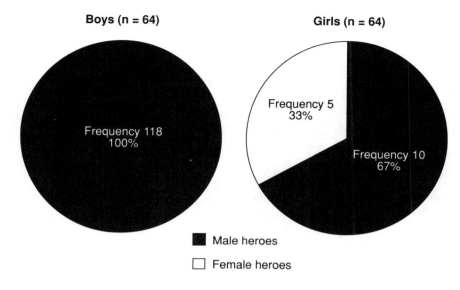

Figure 2.3.   **Gender of boys' and girls' famous athletic heroes from all-walks-of-life questioning.** Data are from the general section of the interview. Note the difference in the total frequency of heroes represented on each chart. Overall frequency = 133.

It is also clear that the boys chose a much higher number of famous athletic heroes. Responding to questions about famous athletes specifically, the total number named by the girls amounted to only 46% of those the boys named (see Figure 2.2). In answering questions about famous heroes from all walks of life, the actual number of athletes chosen by the girls was a minuscule 13% of the total selected by the boys (see Figure 2.3). These results reflect a broader tendency of the girls to choose fewer famous heroes overall. They named only 64% of the total number of famous heroes from all walks of life identified by the boys.

Greater proportions of the famous heroes chosen by the girls were entertainers and political or military leaders (see Figure 2.4). In selecting entertainers, however, the girls still named fewer than the boys, identifying 87% of the boys' total. Political or military leaders were the only group of famous heroes selected in greater numbers by the girls; the boys chose only 73% as many as the girls.

Times are changing, but much evidence remains that boys and men continue to be more interested and involved in sport than girls and women. Perhaps somewhat less disparity exists between the two genders regarding their interest in entertainment and political or military concerns. Not desiring to choose many famous athletes as heroes, girls and women may be left primarily with choices from the other two walks of life.

The proportions of males and females found in the Greensboro study among the three sets of well-known heroes probably reflect the gender proportions in

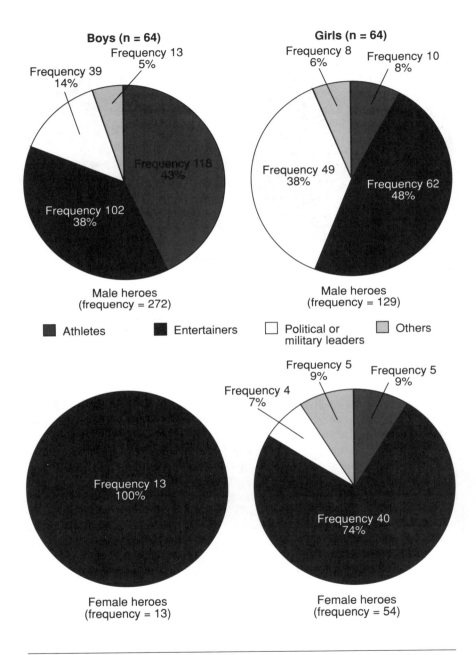

Boys (n = 64)

Frequency 13
5%

Frequency 39
14%

Frequency 118
43%

Frequency 102
38%

Male heroes
(frequency = 272)

Girls (n = 64)

Frequency 8
6%

Frequency 10
8%

Frequency 49
38%

Frequency 62
48%

Male heroes
(frequency = 129)

■ Athletes   ■ Entertainers   □ Political or
military leaders   ▨ Others

Frequency 13
100%

Female heroes
(frequency = 13)

Frequency 5
9%

Frequency 5
9%

Frequency 4
7%

Frequency 40
74%

Female heroes
(frequency = 54)

Figure 2.4.   Walks of life of boys' and girls' famous heroes, by gender of heroes.
Data are from the general section of the interview. Mixed-gender groups and heroes
for whom gender was not determined constituted 1% of boys' choices and 3% of girls'
choices and are not included in this analysis because of their small numbers. Note the
differences in the total frequency of heroes represented on each chart.

the pools of publicly prominent people in these three walks of life in American society in the early 1980s. Throughout the 1980s only small numbers of well-known females had roles in political or military leadership or in athletics. There were many more in entertainment fields, but even here the disparity favored males. Looking specifically at entertainment, the Screen Actors' Guild reports that in 1983 the membership consisted of 56% males and 44% females (personal communication, SAG Public Relations, March 13, 1987). A 1977-78 study of prime-time and Saturday morning fictional television programs found that the characters consisted of 71% males and 29% females (Greenberg, Simmons, Hogan, & Atkin, 1980). For the top 100 best-selling music albums in 1982, 76% of the recording artists were males, 14% were females, and 10% were mixed-gender groups (personal communication, *Billboard* Research Services, February 16, 1993). A small but steady increase in the proportion of female characters on prime-time network television occurred in the 1970s and 1980s; looking collectively at the decade of the 1980s, the characters consisted of about 65% males and 35% females (personal communication, Nancy Signorielli, Department of Communication, University of Delaware, February 16, 1993). The 1980s and early 1990s also showed an increase in the number of female recording artists featured on the top 100 best-selling albums; the figures for 1992 were 69% males, 20% females, and 11% mixed groups (personal communication, *Billboard* Research Services, February 16, 1993). Membership proportions in the Screen Actors' Guild in 1992 were almost identical to those in the early 1980s (personal communication, SAG Public Relations, February 16, 1993).

Considerable evidence suggests that girls and women are more personally, privately, or domestically oriented, while boys and men are more publicly focused (Gamarnikow, Morgan, Purvis, & Taylorson, 1983; Lever, 1976; O'Brien, 1981; Ortner & Whitehead, 1981; Rosaldo, 1974). In line with this, the girls in the Greensboro study selected personal acquaintances as athletic heroes more frequently than the boys did, although the largest percentage of athletic heroes for both the boys and the girls consisted of famous, well-known athletes (see Figure 2.5). The girls selected slightly over one third of their athletic heroes from personal acquaintances; slightly fewer than two thirds were famous public figures. The boys chose somewhat less than one fifth of their athletic heroes from personal acquaintances; slightly over four fifths were famous athletes. Overall, the boys' personally known athletic heroes amounted to only 85% of the total for the girls.

Looking at the gender of the personally known athletic heroes in the Greensboro study, we can see that the girls chose just over 40% females, whereas the boys named almost entirely males (see Figure 2.6). Overall, the boys had almost no female athletic heroes—either famous or personally known (see Figures 2.2 and 2.6). There were also a few others—mixed-gender groups (e.g., parents, groups of friends) and a small number whose gender could not be determined. Although the girls chose few athletic heroes overall, they included more females than the boys did, and about one third of their female athletic heroes were personal acquaintances (see Figures 2.2 and 2.6). If we had looked only at public figures (which is the focus of most other studies), we would have missed this other

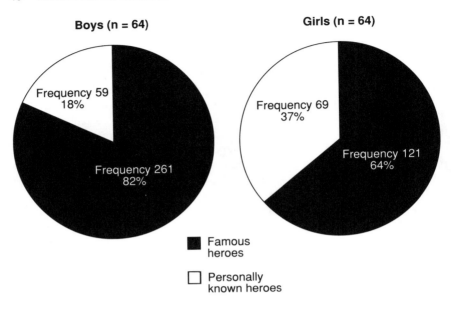

Boys (n = 64)

Frequency 59
18%

Frequency 261
82%

Girls (n = 64)

Frequency 69
37%

Frequency 121
64%

■ Famous
heroes

□ Personally
known heroes

**Figure 2.5.   Boys' and girls' famous and personally known athletic heroes from
sport-only questioning.** Note the difference in the total frequency of heroes
represented on each chart. Overall frequency = 510.

important set of girls' athletic heroes. It is not surprising that a substantial number
of the Greensboro girls' female athletic heroes were personal acquaintances.
There are many more females to choose from in the personal, face-to-face domain
than in public life.

Beyond the larger pool of male athletes in the public domain, and a greater
pool of female athletes in the personal realm, other factors might be contributing
to the selection frequencies observed above. The findings are consistent with the
scholarly literature concerning modeling (Bandura, 1969, 1971a, 1971b) and
reference others (Hyman, 1975; Hyman & Singer, 1968; Schmitt, 1972). These
lines of research are concerned with what influences people to imitate or model
the actions of others. These processes have been examined within two major
theoretical frameworks. Modeling has been examined by social psychologists
primarily in laboratory settings, and reference-other influences have been studied
primarily by sociologists in field settings. To copy others one must obviously
first attend to them and observe their actions. Evidence shows that people are
more likely to be imitated when they have high status relative to observers,
similarity to observers, nurturing qualities, or other characteristics that observers
find admirable. We can also assume that they are more likely to be attended to
in the first place under these conditions, and this is the tie between the selection
frequencies reported here and the modeling and reference-other processes. The
findings presented above can be considered in terms of this conceptual framework.

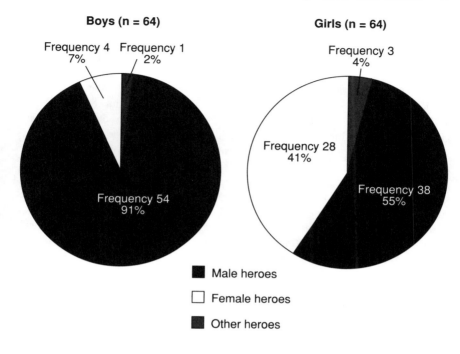

Figure 2.6.   Gender of boys' and girls' personally known athletic heroes from sport-only questioning. Note the difference in the total frequency of heroes represented on each chart. Overall frequency = 128. "Other heroes" are mixed-gender groups and heroes whose gender could not be determined.

First we will consider people's selections of well-known athletic heroes. Males are generally thought to have higher status in American society than females (Frieze, Parsons, Johnson, Ruble, & Zellman, 1978). This may contribute to the higher selection rate of male athletes by both men and boys, and women and girls. In addition, however, men and boys would also tend to select male athletes as heroes because of their same-sex similarity. Women and girls, on the other hand, would have only the high status of male athletes as an attraction toward selecting them; they might also be attracted toward female athletic heroes because of same-sex similarity. The athletic hero selection findings we have just examined show that men and boys tend to select primarily male athletic heroes, while women and girls tend to select a number of females among an overall preponderance of males. This is what would be expected under the conditions just outlined.

Turning to personally known athletic heroes, we must remember that in addition to status and similarity attributes, personal acquaintances also typically dispense nurturance and other rewards directly to their admirers. They are often caretaking adults or peers with whom respondents enjoy spending leisure time.

The attraction of the higher status of males may be overcome somewhat in the personal realm by the nurturance and other rewards given out by females (e.g., mothers, teachers, grandmothers). This may account partially for the more visible presence of females among personally known athletic heroes.

In summary, youths' athletic hero choices are tied in a number of ways to gender differences. Overall, girls choose fewer athletic heroes than do boys. Male athletes are selected much more often than female athletes by both genders, but girls include more females among their athletic heroes than do boys. There is a substantial proportion of female athletes among personally known athletic heroes, and these are chosen more often by girls. Among public, well-known heroes, girls focus more on entertainers and political or military leaders, partially compensating for their selection of fewer athletes. In terms of the debate, these differences suggest that athletic heroes have compartmentalized appeal along gender lines. These findings can be fruitfully considered in light of proportions of males and females in the pools of potential heroes in society, boys' and girls' different levels of interest and involvement in sport, and modeling and reference-other processes.

Race Comparisons: Blacks and Whites

Black and white athletes predominate in elite sport in American society, although other racial and ethnic groups are certainly represented. Most of the research on American sport that deals with racial and ethnic minorities concerns blacks. For these reasons comparisons of hero choices based on race are limited to considerations of black and white youths. Much of the evidence in this section comes from the Greensboro study. The racial make-up of the respondents in that investigation was purposely limited to blacks and whites because of the large preponderance of the two groups in the region (see Appendix A).

The race comparisons presented here pertain primarily to famous athletic heroes, not personal acquaintances. Scant evidence exists regarding race of personally known athletic heroes. Although personal acquaintances were examined in the Greensboro study, we did not ask the race of such individuals due to concerns about biasing answers, and independent assessment was not feasible (see Appendix A). We know only that the athletic heroes chosen by both the black and white youngsters consisted of about three fourths famous athletes and one fourth personal acquaintances.

Before proceeding we need also to remember that there is a socioeconomic gap between blacks and whites in American society—blacks are overrepresented among the poor, and whites are overrepresented among the wealthy. Although socioeconomic status has not been examined to any great extent in connection with youths' hero choices, it has been shown to be an important factor in many aspects of social life; therefore, the socioeconomic difference between blacks and whites should be kept in mind. In the Greensboro study, a comparison of the education levels of the youths' parents (one of several commonly used indicators of socioeconomic status) suggests that the blacks came from less advantaged socioeconomic backgrounds than the whites (see Appendix A).

Results of several polls show that black athletes comprise a substantial portion of the famous players youths consider praiseworthy, but that whites still predominate. Blacks account for about one third of adolescents' most frequently chosen athletic heroes ("The Top Ten," 1977); 41% of the total array of praise-worthy athletes selected by a sample of black and white college students, and one third of the most frequently selected of these (Vander Velden, 1986); one half of the praiseworthy athletes chosen most often by a national sample of secondary school students ("Heroes of Young," 1980); and about one third of the entire array of favorite athletes selected by a racially heterogeneous group of youths and adults (Miller Brewing Company, 1983). Most of the remaining athletes selected in these studies are whites.

In these polls blacks appear in larger percentages than we would expect relative to their proportion in the overall United States population—about 11.8% at the time of the studies (U.S. Bureau of the Census, 1984). Even so, the proportions of black athletes in these investigations may not have equalled their numbers in the overall pool of elite athletes seen by the public in the early 1980s. In 1980 blacks comprised 75% of the players in professional basketball and 22% of those in professional baseball, and in 1982 nearly 49% of professional football players were black (Coakley, 1986, p. 145). These figures did not change much in the later 1980s. In 1988, 21% of professional baseball players and 57% of professional football players were black; in 1989 black professional basketball players comprised 73% of the total (Coakley, 1990, p. 208).

In partial contrast to the surveys showing large proportions of white athletes selected by both black and white respondents, Vander Velden (1986) reports that two thirds to three fourths of both black and white college students chose same-race athletic heroes. For the white respondents, this is consistent with the other surveys. However, the larger proportion of black athletes chosen by black respondents is incongruent. Most of the other polls probably involved relatively broad-based samples, and in such cases white respondents would clearly be in the majority. If people tend to select same-race athletic heroes, then a preponderance of white respondents would overload the group of chosen heroes with whites.

However this possibility was not upheld by evidence from the Greensboro study, where there was a stronger focus on black athletic heroes than in most other investigations. When the respondents were asked to identify famous athletic heroes, almost three fourths of those named by the black youngsters and just under one half of those named by the white youngsters were blacks (see Figure 2.7). A small number of others consisted of racially mixed groups (e.g., a whole team, or a portion of a team), people with racial identities other than black or white, and a few individuals whose race could not be determined. When asked to name famous heroes from all walks of life, the athletic heroes selected by both the black and white youths consisted of about two thirds blacks and one third whites (see Figure 2.8). The larger proportions of famous black athletes named by the Greensboro youths may be closer to the actual percentages of famous black players receiving regular public exposure in the early 1980s.

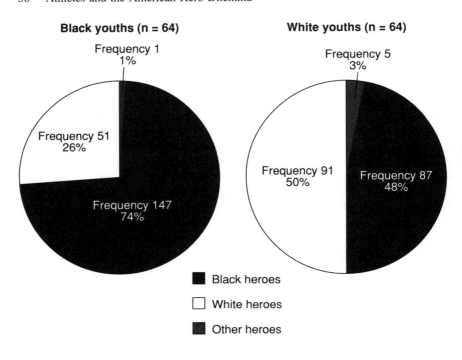

Figure 2.7.   Race of black and white youths' famous athletic heroes from sport-only questioning. Note the difference in the total frequency of heroes represented on each chart. Overall frequency = 382. "Other heroes" are mixed-race groups, racial identities other than black or white, and heroes whose race could not be determined.

Research suggests that blacks are more strongly oriented toward sport than whites. Athletics seem more central in their lives (Rudman, 1986; Spreitzer & Snyder, 1990). If blacks are more extensively involved in sport, we might expect a larger number of athletic hero selections by black respondents, and there was a small tendency in this direction in the Greensboro study. When asked specifically to identify famous athletic heroes, the actual number of people named by the white youths was 92% of the number named by the blacks (see Figure 2.7). In response to a more general request for names of famous heroes from all walks of life, the actual number of athletes included by the white youths was 75% of the number included by the blacks (see Figure 2.8).

However, these percentages must be set in the context of the choices of other famous heroes named by the Greensboro youths. Overall, the actual number of famous heroes from all walks of life identified by the white respondents was 83% of those named by the blacks (see Figure 2.9). The whites named only 64% of the total entertainers named by the blacks, an even smaller ratio than for athletes. The only group of famous heroes chosen more frequently by the white youths was political or military leaders—the black respondents named only 67%

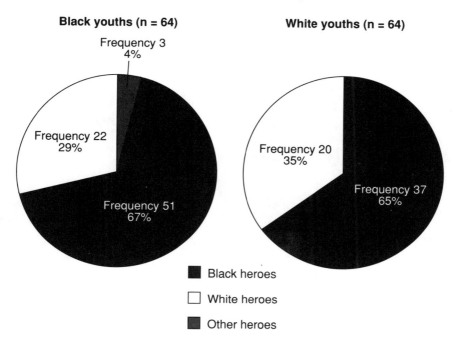

Black youths (n = 64)

Frequency 3
4%

Frequency 22
29%

Frequency 51
67%

White youths (n = 64)

Frequency 20
35%

Frequency 37
65%

■ Black heroes

☐ White heroes

■ Other heroes

Figure 2.8.   Race of black and white youths' famous athletic heroes from all-walks-of-life questioning. Data are from the general section of the interview. Note the difference in the total frequency of heroes represented on each chart. Overall frequency = 133. "Other heroes" are mixed-race groups, racial identities other than black or white, and heroes whose race could not be determined.

of the number identified by the whites. These figures indicate that both athletes and entertainers were more prominent for the black youths than for the whites, with entertainers being even more prominent than athletes.

The proportions of black and white athletes participating in the major professional sports in the United States in the early 1980s can be contrasted with the proportions of black and white entertainers and political or military leaders. Looking first at entertainers, in 1977-78 there were 9% blacks and 86% whites among the characters in prime-time and Saturday morning fictional television programs (Greenberg et al., 1980). The Screen Actors' Guild membership in 1983 consisted of 88% whites and 6% blacks (personal communication, SAG Public Relations, March 13, 1987). Among the top 100 best-selling music albums in 1982, 83% featured white recording artists while 17% featured blacks (personal communication, *Billboard* Research Services, February 16, 1993). Clearly, in the early 1980s the overall percentage of famous black entertainers was not as great as the overall percentage of blacks among well-known athletes.

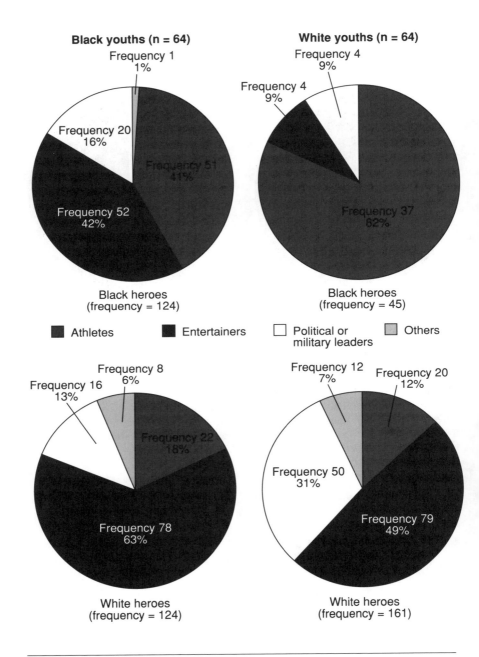

Black youths (n = 64)

Frequency 1
1%

Frequency 20
16%

Frequency 51
41%

Frequency 52
42%

Black heroes
(frequency = 124)

White youths (n = 64)

Frequency 4
9%

Frequency 4
9%

Frequency 37
82%

Black heroes
(frequency = 45)

■ Athletes   ■ Entertainers   ☐ Political or   ▨ Others
                                    military leaders

Frequency 8
6%

Frequency 16
13%

Frequency 22
18%

Frequency 78
63%

White heroes
(frequency = 124)

Frequency 12
7%

Frequency 20
12%

Frequency 50
31%

Frequency 79
49%

White heroes
(frequency = 161)

Figure 2.9. Walks of life of black and white youths' famous heroes, by race of heroes. Data are from the general section of the interview. Racially mixed groups and heroes other than black or white constituted 4% of black youths' choices and 6% of white youths' choices and are not included in this analysis because of their small numbers. Note the differences in the total frequencies of heroes represented on each chart.

Comparing these numbers with those from more recent years, we can see a shift toward a somewhat greater number of prominent black singers and musicians. In 1992 the recording artists featured on the top 100 best-selling albums included 72% whites and 27% blacks, a 59% increase in blacks since 1982 (personal communication, *Billboard* Research Services, February 16, 1993). However, the figures for motion picture and television actors remained similar to those of the early 1980s. In the fall of 1992 the Screen Actors' Guild membership included 85% whites and 9% blacks (personal communication, SAG Public Relations, February 16, 1993). For prime-time network television characters, similar percentages have been reported throughout the 1970s and 1980s—about 90% whites and 10% blacks and other minorities (personal communication, Nancy Signorielli, Department of Communication, University of Delaware, February 16, 1993).

There were also few black political or military leaders in the 1980s. Throughout the decade, for example, all U.S. senators were white, and the U.S. House of Representatives varied between 92% and 95% white membership (U.S. Bureau of the Census, 1992). From 1982 to 1983 President Reagan's cabinet included 100% whites, while 10 years later President Bush's cabinet included 88% whites and 6% blacks. Blacks such as politician Jesse Jackson, military leader Colin Powell, and various big-city mayors became more prominent in the later 1980s, but they were still a small minority.

With these differences in mind, we can examine more closely the race of the famous athletes, entertainers, and political or military leaders selected as heroes by the youths in the Greensboro study. Turning first to political or military leaders: With a rather small pool of blacks to choose from, it is not surprising that few appeared among the youths' black heroes. Nevertheless, the black youths tended to have a more balanced number of black and white political or military leaders, while the white youths chose almost exclusively whites in this category (see Figure 2.9). Some of the black political heroes were outside of the formal government, and quite a few of the black youths' choices fell into this category (Martin Luther King, Jr., for example).

Moving to athletes and entertainers, both the black and white respondents chose a lot of black athletes, as we saw above (see Figures 2.7, 2.8, and 2.9). By contrast, both racial groups chose a larger proportion of white entertainers (see Figure 2.9). Results of several national polls of secondary school students in the 1980s and early 1990s support this greater emphasis on white entertainers and black athletes (see Table 2.3, pages 30 and 31) ("Heroes of Young," 1980, 1981, 1985-1991).

It is clear, however, that the black youths also attended fairly heavily to black entertainers (see Figure 2.9). Among their famous black heroes were about equal proportions of black entertainers and black athletes. Proportions for the whites' choices of same-race athletes and entertainers were not as similar, favoring entertainers. Although the proportions were uneven, however, the white youths' choices of white heroes were more widely distributed between athletes and entertainers than were their choices of black heroes. The latter consisted almost entirely of black athletes.

As we know, in the 1980s a high proportion of famous athletes were black, and a high proportion of famous entertainers were white. This may be the major factor behind the tendency of the Greensboro youths to name more black athletes and more white entertainers. In addition, however, a lingering racial stereotype rooted in notions of black superiority in athletics may have been at work. Racist, stereotypic views of blacks in American society have emphasized their physical superiority and mental inferiority in relation to whites. Those who perceive famous blacks and whites through this distorted lens might select more black athletic heroes because of their physical superiority. Similarly, they might be less inclined to select black entertainers.

In the Greensboro study, the black youths clearly selected a balanced set of black heroes that included many athletes, entertainers, and political or military leaders (see Figure 2.9). By comparison, the white youths included slightly over 80% athletes among their black heroes. However, the white youths chose a more balanced set of white heroes that included quite a few athletes, entertainers, and political or military leaders. By comparison, the black youths named almost two thirds entertainers among their white heroes. So, both the black and white youths chose somewhat skewed sets of opposite-race heroes and more balanced sets of same-race heroes—which is what we would expect if traditional, stereotypic views of blacks and whites are operating.

In terms of hero choice evidence, the most likely places to look for suggestions of racial stereotyping would be in white youths' choices of black heroes, and black youths' choices of white heroes. It seems reasonable to suggest that the overwhelming focus on athletes among the black heroes selected by the white youths reflects lingering stereotypic views of blacks. The whites seem to have ignored most other sorts of black heroes to focus on a small core of physically gifted athletes. By the same token, the slightly heavier focus on white entertainers by the black youngsters may reflect a modest level of stereotypic perception of whites. In relation to the other famous white heroes, the proportions of white athletes selected by both the black and white youths were relatively small, which is also in line with stereotypic thinking suggesting white physical inferiority. Later, it will be important to note whether stereotyped beliefs are evident in the Greensboro youths' characterizations of their heroes.

Let's look at the findings just discussed in the context of the literature concerning modeling (Bandura, 1969, 1971a, 1971b) and reference others (Hyman, 1975; Hyman & Singer, 1968; Schmitt, 1972). Relatively little research exists on the influence of race, but some of the factors found to operate more generally seem likely to be important in relation to racial characteristics. Recall that people with high status and those with whom a potential imitator has similarity are more likely to be copied than people with low status and those with greater dissimilarity. Thus, we might expect whites to attend strongly to white models on both counts. Blacks might be likely to attend to whites for their high status, and to blacks for their similarity. So we might expect to see a clearer-cut selection of white athletic heroes by white youths, and a more mixed selection of black and white athletic heroes by black youths, similar to boys' selection of many male heroes and girls' somewhat more mixed selection of male and female heroes.

Based on modeling and reference-other processes, we would expect black youths to select a lot of black athletic heroes due to the similarity factor, but also some whites due to the generally higher status of whites in American society (though an exception might apply in the case of athletes; more on this soon). The Greensboro findings and Vander Velden's (1986) results showing high (but not exclusive) same-race selections by black respondents are consistent with this expectation. Along the same lines, we would expect white youths to select mostly white athletic heroes because of both their similarity and their higher status. Vander Velden's finding of high (but not exclusive) same-race selections by white respondents supports this. However, the Greensboro evidence is contradictory. The white youths' choices of famous athletes included between one half and two thirds black players, and black athletes were predominant among the full set of famous black heroes they selected from all walks of life (see Figures 2.7, 2.8, and 2.9).

One other factor should be considered from the standpoint of the modeling and reference-other framework. Perhaps black athletes are perceived by young people to have higher status or prestige than white athletes. If this is the case, then black youths should select almost entirely black athletes and very few whites (due to their high status combined with similarity), and white respondents should select a mixture of black and white athletes (due to high status combined with dissimilarity). Vander Velden's (1986) data are congruent with the prediction for black respondents, but not for whites. The Greensboro data are somewhat more congruent (but not entirely so) with this prediction for both blacks and whites (see Figures 2.7 and 2.8).

Looking at choices of entertainers and political or military leaders, a strong trend was shown toward white youths selecting primarily white heroes and black youths selecting a mixture of black and white heroes. (Compare the frequencies in Figure 2.9.) These findings are congruent with expectations based on modeling and reference-other processes. We must keep in mind, however, that the overall pools of famous entertainers and political or military leaders in American society in the 1980s consisted of a preponderance of whites, and the availability of greater proportions of whites in these two walks of life may have influenced these selection patterns.

In summary, a number of racial differences exist regarding youths' choices of famous athletic heroes. Blacks name a larger number of athletic heroes than do whites. Nevertheless, both black and white respondents choose a preponderance of blacks among athletic heroes. Comparing their total sets of black heroes, however, white youths select a very high proportion of black athletes, while blacks choose a more balanced set of athletes, entertainers, and political or military leaders. White heroes named by whites are somewhat more balanced among athletes, entertainers, and political or military leaders than are their black heroes. White heroes named by blacks are somewhat skewed toward a greater number of entertainers. White youths include mostly whites among entertainers and political or military leaders, while black youths name a mixture of blacks and whites. In relation to the debate, these differences point toward the possibility that athletic heroes have somewhat compartmentalized appeal in terms of black and white racial groups. It is worthwhile to consider these findings in light of proportions of blacks and whites in the pools of potential heroes in American society, different levels of interest and involvement in sport by blacks and whites, modeling and reference-other processes, relative status or prestige accorded to black and white athletes, and racial stereotyping.

Grade Comparisons

Earlier we saw that children and adolescents tend to admire athletes and entertainers, whereas adults are more oriented toward political leaders. Athletes and entertainers are associated with major performative genres in American society that have make-believe—some would say frivolous and shallow—qualities about them. Politicians, on the other hand, seem more closely associated with the seriousness of ongoing life. This difference may partially account for the shift in focus on hero types from childhood to adulthood.

We can speculate, however, that the lower numbers of well-known athletes and entertainers chosen by adults probably represent only one side of a ∩-shaped curve. Increasing cognitive complexity throughout childhood and increasing exposure to people and events beyond the family make it likely that the number of famous athletes and entertainers chosen as praiseworthy would increase as children get older. Then at some point they would begin to decline to the levels observed in adults. It is unclear what might happen with political leaders. The frequency with which they are chosen might undergo a steady increase through childhood and adolescence, or there might be some other pattern.

The Greensboro study is the main source of evidence pertaining to these matters. It provides cross-sectional data about differences in hero choices among 3rd, 6th, 9th, and 12th graders and includes information about choices of famous athletes as well as personally known ones. Because of concerns about biasing answers, the respondents were not asked to provide their heroes' ages (see Appendix A). Instead, a rough indication of age was obtained by distinguishing whether or not a hero was out of high school. This produced two categories of heroes—youths (still in high school or earlier grades) and adults (out of high school).

When asked specifically to name well-known athletic heroes, the youths at all four grade levels named adults almost exclusively (see Figure 2.10). This is not surprising because almost all famous athletes in American society are beyond high school age. Age proportions for the famous athletic heroes named in response to questioning about heroes from all walks of life were not calculated because there were not enough heroes chosen by each of the four grade-level groups to make such an analysis meaningful.

Also, as might be expected, the respondents identified rather large proportions of youths in response to a specific request to name heroic personal acquaintances involved in athletics (see Figure 2.11). As we saw earlier, the overall number of heroic personal acquaintances involved in athletics was not very great. Clearly, however, if youths are selected as athletic heroes they will come primarily from personal acquaintances because there are very few in the pool of famous athletes. The proportions of adult and youth heroes are about the same for the 3rd, 9th, and 12th graders but there was an unusually large number of others among the 6th graders' choices, making their data difficult to compare; others included mixed-age groups (e.g., family, a baseball team) along with a few heroes whose ages could not be determined.

Although greater availability of both famous adult athletes and personally known young athletes is probably most important for explaining the selection patterns just noted, modeling (Bandura, 1969, 1971a, 1971b) and reference-other (Hyman, 1975; Hyman & Singer, 1968; Schmitt, 1972) processes might also be operating. We can only speculate about this possibility because no evidence is available to address it directly. Age similarities between respondents and their young athletic friends, as well as the rewarding nature of their friendships, might lead to selection of similar-aged young people as heroes. On the other hand, the relatively high status of adults and their ability to bestow nurturance and other rewards might orient admirers of all ages toward adult heroes. These factors probably interact in complex ways that are hard to predict.

Among the heroes chosen in response to specific questioning about sport, a definite increase appeared in the actual number of famous athletes selected as heroes in the middle grades (6th and 9th) (see Figure 2.12). By comparison, a relatively constant number of choices of personal acquaintances was present across all four grade levels. This inflated frequency of famous athletes in the middle grades resulted in larger percentages of famous athletes relative to personal acquaintances. Famous athletic heroes were especially salient for the middle-graders.

These findings can be interpreted in the following way. The 3rd graders, with somewhat limited exposure and attentiveness to the world beyond their own families, probably had a smaller pool of famous athletes to draw from. The youths in the other grades, with much more extensive exposure to sport on television and perhaps live attendance at major sporting events, had a much larger pool of well-known athletes to draw from and perhaps also more finely honed affective attachments to sport. However, the 12th graders may have reached the point where concerns about the distant world of popular athletics were somewhat blunted by growing complexities in their daily lives. In addition, the continued selection of personally known athletic heroes at all four grade levels indicates that although the youths in the middle grades showed heightened interest in well-known athletes, they did not abandon personally known athletic heroes.

We can also compare the relative proportions of famous athletes, entertainers, and political or military leaders selected at each of the four grade levels (see

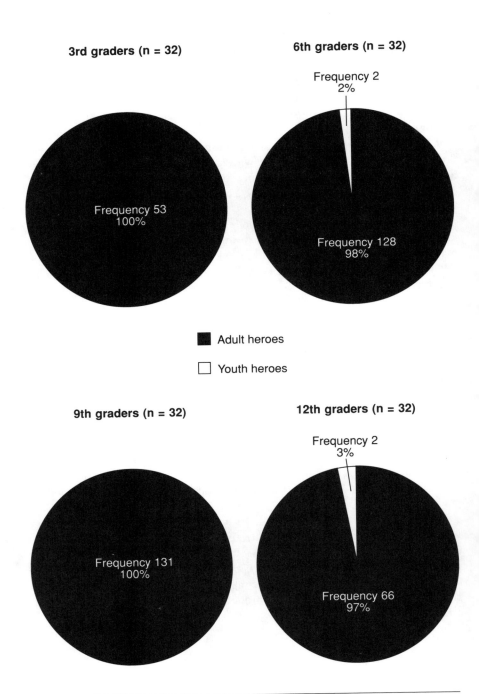

Figure 2.10. Age of famous athletic heroes of youths from four grade levels: sport-only questioning. Note the differences in the total frequencies of heroes represented on each chart. Overall frequency = 382.

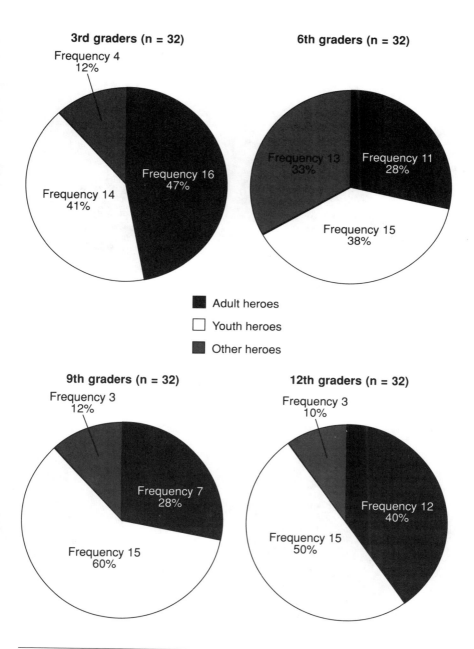

3rd graders (n = 32)

Frequency 4
12%

Frequency 16
47%

Frequency 14
41%

6th graders (n = 32)

Frequency 13
33%

Frequency 11
28%

Frequency 15
38%

■ Adult heroes
□ Youth heroes
■ Other heroes

9th graders (n = 32)

Frequency 3
12%

Frequency 7
28%

Frequency 15
60%

12th graders (n = 32)

Frequency 3
10%

Frequency 12
40%

Frequency 15
50%

Figure 2.11. Age of personally known athletic heroes of youths from four grade levels: sport-only questioning. Note the differences in the total frequencies of heroes represented on each chart. Overall frequency = 128. ''Other heroes'' are mixed-age groups and heroes whose age could not be determined.

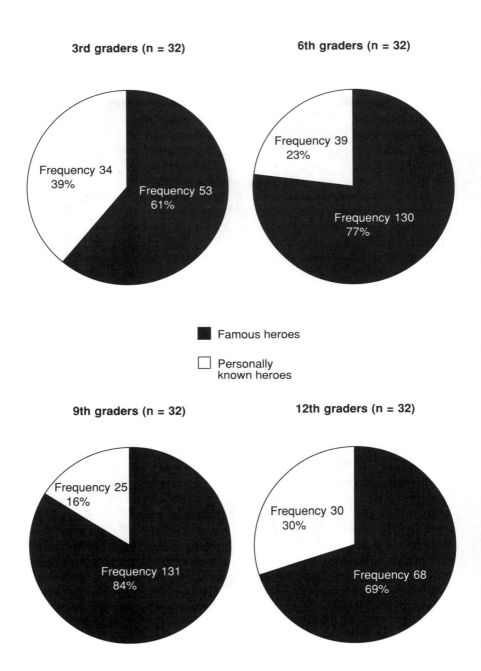

Figure 2.12. Famous and personally known athletic heroes of youths from four grade levels: sport-only questioning. Note the differences in the total frequencies of heroes represented on each chart. Overall frequency = 510.

Figure 2.13). Over three fourths of the 3rd graders' famous heroes were entertainers, while in the more advanced grades entertainers accounted for only about one third to one half of the totals. We might speculate that the heavy choice of entertainers by the 3rd graders stemmed from watching television. Although one can learn about athletics and political or military activities from watching television, apparently the entertainers were most salient to the 3rd graders. It should also be noted that the younger children named quite a few cartoon characters as heroes, and these were included in the entertainer group. The proportion of entertainers decreased in the middle grades, accompanied by larger percentages of athletes and political or military leaders. Finally, by the 12th grade the combined proportion of athletes and entertainers was just over one half of the total, while the combined proportion of political or military leaders and others (e.g., humanitarians, explorers, scientists) was just under one half. The 12th graders gravitated more toward people who dealt with crucial concerns of a complex world—political or military leaders and other sorts of problem-solvers—forgetting some of the athletes and entertainers selected more often by the younger children.

In summary, youths' choices of athletic heroes differ in several ways across grade levels. One similarity is evident, however: Almost all famous athletic heroes are adults, and a substantial proportion of personally known athletic heroes are youths. There is a pronounced increase in the number of famous athletes named by middle graders; coupled with a more constant number of personal acquaintances across the four grade levels, this results in a greater proportion of famous heroic athletes in the middle grades. Looking more specifically at famous heroes from all walks of life, a shift occurs from heavy emphasis on entertainers in the 3rd grade, to moderate attention to political or military leaders in the middle grades, to an approximately even emphasis on two groups in the 12th grade: (a) entertainers and athletes and (b) political or military leaders and others. Considering the debate, this evidence points toward the possibility of compartmentalized appeal of athletic heroes among young people at different grade levels. We can place these findings in the context of the number of adults/youths in the pools of potential heroes in American society, greater interest among older adolescents in crucial concerns of a complex world and growing complexities in their own lives, increasing cognitive complexity and wider involvement in society as young people grow up, and modeling and reference-other processes.

Summary and Implications: Gender, Race, and Grade Comparisons

The evidence concerning gender, race, and grade comparisons, although limited in generalizability because it comes almost exclusively from the Greensboro study, provides initial information about compartmentalization. However, these aspects of athletic hero choices are not particularly helpful in resolving the debate because they can be used to the advantage of either side. Still, such evidence enhances insights about diversities and similarities in youths' hero selections, and the value of such information for helping us to learn about the multifaceted nature of American society may override this drawback.

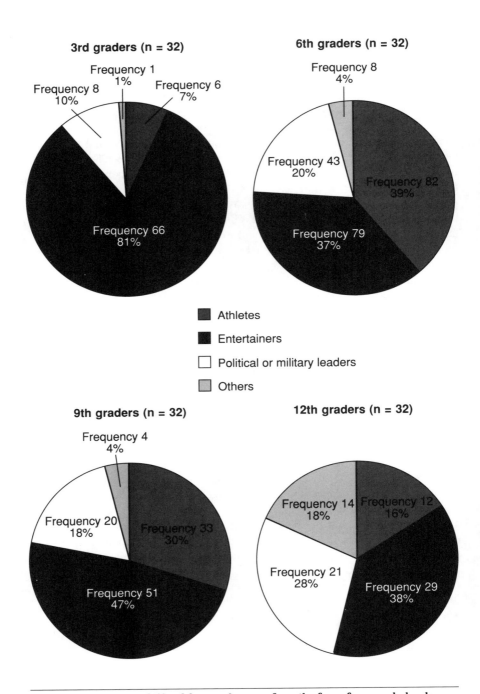

Figure 2.13. Walks of life of famous heroes of youths from four grade levels.
Data are from the general section of the interview. Note the differences in the total
frequencies of heroes represented on each chart. Overall frequency = 477.

The athletic heroes with broadest appeal may be famous black males. Male athletes are chosen in large numbers by both boys and girls, and black athletes are selected frequently by both black and white youths. We must be careful not to generalize too far here, of course. On the one hand, black basketball star Michael Jordan has the longest recent record for inclusion on an annual list of heroes selected from all walks of life (see Table 2.3, pages 30 and 31). On the other hand, black boxer Muhammad Ali was identified by college students as the most frequently liked *and* the most frequently disliked athletic star (Vander Velden, 1986).

Athletic heroes with the narrowest appeal may be personally known females. Although they are chosen occasionally by both boys and girls, especially by girls, their numbers are small. Furthermore, the appeal of any particular personal acquaintance is limited to a relatively small network of people.

Future research should examine in more detail the factors that underlie differences in the selection of heroes. These factors include

- the nature of the pools of people from which they are selected,
- levels of interest and involvement in athletics on the part of particular groups of admirers,
- admirers' increasing cognitive complexity and involvement in society as they grow up,
- relative status or prestige of different groups of athletes,
- various kinds of stereotyping, and
- modeling and reference-other processes.

In addition, more fine-grained studies are needed in which interactions among such factors as gender, race, age/grade, social class, sexual preference, ethnicity, geographic region, and rural/urban differences are considered. One approach would be to focus on specific social formations such as Japanese girls in Los Angeles, youngsters in Appalachia, or members of a New York inner-city gang. Also, boys who go against broader trends and select one or more female athletic heroes might be interesting to study.

Looking more broadly beyond gender, race, and grade comparisons to reflect once again on the entire range of evidence about athletic hero choices, it is clear that the data provide only limited information about shallowness, flawed complexity, and compartmentalization. In an effort to overcome this limitation, we turn next to examine youths' characterizations of athletic heroes.

Chapter 3

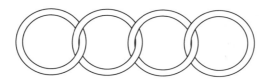

Youths' Characterizations of Heroic Athletes

We have seen that examining youths' athletic hero choices moves us only modestly toward resolution of the debate. To gain further headway we need to look at the ways these chosen heroes are characterized by their admirers. We'll use this information to address all three points of contention—shallowness, flawed complexity, and compartmentalization—but most of the available data pertain to shallowness.

A small amount of evidence is also available concerning flawed complexity. If defined in a way that minimizes its potential to support both sides, then this characteristic can be useful in helping to settle the debate. The key is to look at the extent to which respondents themselves judge their heroes to be flawed, rather than relying on independent evaluations made by pessimistic or optimistic external analysts.

We also have some scattered evidence concerning compartmentalization. This consists of scant information about differences among specific groups of admirers regarding the ways athletic heroes are characterized. Knowledge of compartmentalization remains less helpful in resolving the debate, however, because both sides can use it to their advantage. Pessimistically, compartmentalization suggests the demise of traditional athletic heroes in a troubled society. Optimistically, it serves to buttress the idea of the continued existence of a multiplicity of athletic heroes in a vital society open to self-criticism and growth.

Findings concerning youths' conceptions of athletic heroes are not used much to argue either position in the debate—obviously because of lack of research. Investigations have focused primarily on hero choices. Furthermore, the small amount of information on hero characterizations available in the past was not very detailed. I hope that evidence from the 1982 Greensboro study will shed more light on the ways that young people view the athletes they identify as heroes. But because most of the available evidence is from the Greensboro study, we must be cautious not to overgeneralize. Before turning to this investigation, however, let's first examine information from other research.

Hero Characterizations in Other Studies

The scholarly literature dealing with characteristics of praiseworthy athletes spans many disciplines, including history, folklore and literary studies, communication studies, and the social and behavioral sciences. Analysts often use their own personal opinions along with data from sources such as biographies, novels, short stories, folklore, and the mass media to identify qualities of a wide array of highly admired athletes, some of whom are labeled heroes. Specific athletes are often compared and contrasted. Although this work is interesting, it is rather far afield from our present concerns because it does not deal directly with the general public's conceptions of the athletes they consider praiseworthy.

Our discussion here will be limited to investigations emphasizing the latter, in which people's opinions about those they selected were directly assessed, usually through surveys and interviews. The central concerns of these studies vary somewhat. Respondents were not always asked to discuss heroes specifically; some questioning asked for the most admired or favorite person, the most influential person, or the person a respondent would most like to emulate. Unfortunately, the total body of work is too small to compare meaningfully the results from these different approaches. We will, however, distinguish investigations emphasizing heroes from those focused on highly admired people not identified specifically as heroic.

Several relatively broad investigations provide a context in which to situate other work dealing with athletes. These more comprehensive studies focus on people's conceptions of praiseworthy individuals from many walks of life. Klapp (1962) asked college students to develop a large set of "social types"—commonly shared role models in American society. The students were given long lists of slang descriptions of people that they "augmented, defined and rated" (Klapp, 1956, p. 337). They classified the role models that emerged as either heroes, villains, or fools. These were anonymous social types not tied to specific individuals; however, in the course of developing them, specific people were named as examples. Sometimes these individuals' characteristics did not fit neatly into one category, and in such cases they were placed into other categories as well. Klapp (1956, 1962) himself then developed subgroups of social types within each of the three broad sets. His final set of heroic types was based on a combination of opinions of college students and his own comparisons of the social types they developed.

His five subgroups of heroes are winners, splendid performers, independent spirits, heroes of social acceptability, and group servants. According to Klapp (1962, pp. 27-28), winners display "getting what you want, beating everybody, being a champ"; splendid performers reflect "shining before an audience, making a 'hit' "; independent spirits are known for "standing alone, making one's way by oneself"; heroes of social acceptability are viewed as "being liked, attractive, good, or otherwise personally acceptable to groups and epitomizing the pleasures of belonging''; and group servants are recognized for ''helping people, cooperation, and self-sacrifice—group service and solidarity.''

Within this framework athletes are usually considered splendid performers; only a few are seen as winners. Splendid performers are admired because they put on a good show; they are known mostly for the surface features of their showmanship rather than for substantive characteristics. Athletes classified as winners are limited to ''strong men'' who win by brute force—boxers in particular. Klapp (1962) believes that putting on a good performance does not necessarily entail winning (p. 35); nevertheless he tags as splendid performers a host of consistently victorious athletes including Babe Ruth, Joe Louis, Babe Zaharias, Jackie Robinson, Maureen Connolly, and Mickey Mantle.

Klapp (1962) provides no rationale for why so few athletes are deemed winners, but his classifications may be tied to his pessimistic stance concerning the demise of heroes in American society. Klapp considers sport a prime site for displays by shallow celebrities; consequently, he may be inclined to classify athletes as splendid performers with little to offer beyond the attractive surface features of well-conditioned bodies and outstanding movement skills.

This is not a completely satisfactory answer, however, because Klapp (1962) condemns all five heroic types, claiming that their traditionally heroic greatness has been substantially curtailed. Winners, along with all the others, are diminished. In his view heroes must have depth of character demonstrated by high intellect and wisdom, high moral standards, consistency in portrayal of ''basic values or roles required of all'' (p. 123), and outstanding achievements (pp. 95-156). These qualities are not merely superficial but internalized as part of the hero's self. People held in high regard merely for their fame, good looks, or appealing smile are not heroes within Klapp's (1962) idealized, archetypical model. Even group servants, who might be thought to possess traditional heroic qualities, have degenerated into meddlers and do-gooders who put on an outward display of goodwill but are not truly good underneath (p. 123).

In another broad study Csikszentmihalyi and Lyons (1982) identify frequently mentioned reasons for admiring people. They interviewed a cross-generational sample of adults and children and found that most reasons can be divided into two clusters: (1) personal competence characteristics (courage, expertise, intellect, strength to carry through with plans, creativity, and versatility); and (2) prosocial characteristics (affection, generosity, social ideals, family devotion, dependability, character, and honesty). Prosocial qualities center on social supportiveness and are more frequently admired in family members, whereas personal competence deals with individual expertise and is admired about equally often in family members and public figures. Overall, highly admired public figures are characterized more often by personal competence, while family members are perceived with more robust characterizations involving both personal competence and prosocial qualities. This is partially confirmed by McCormack's (1984) study of the most influential people in teenagers' lives. Although the study tells us little about public figures (because most of the influential people named by respondents are personal acquaintances), she found that influential personal acquaintances are perceived to be both competent and socially supportive.

Somewhat contradictory results were obtained in two large national surveys of American secondary school students ("Heroes of Young," 1987, 1988). Respondents were asked to identify the most important characteristics of famous people they named as admirable or heroic. Eight of the most common characteristics are the same in both surveys. Seven can be placed in one or the other of the two categories developed by Csikszentmihalyi and Lyons (1982): Three concern personal competence (intelligent, brave, and daring), and four are prosocial qualities (honest, funny, responsible, and cool). This almost even split suggests nearly equal attention to admiration of personal competence and prosocial characteristics, data that are in contrast to respondents' rather one-sided emphasis on personal competence of public figures in the work of Csikszentmihalyi and Lyons. Methodological and sampling differences probably account for some of the difference.

In terms of the debate about the demise of heroes in American society, evidence from Csikszentmihalyi and Lyons (1982), McCormack (1984), and the two national surveys ("Heroes of Young," 1987, 1988) shows that respondents do not often characterize praiseworthy people in shallow ways and stress surface features. Instead they emphasize personal competence and prosocial qualities that highlight much of the traditional vigor thought by the pessimists to have disappeared from our conceptions of heroes. These results clearly support the optimistic position.

Somewhat at odds, however, is Kahn's (1979) evidence demonstrating that for male high school seniors a cluster of characteristics centered on the combined qualities of wealth and fame was second among the five most frequently mentioned qualities of famous, well-known heroes. The other four qualities concern primarily personal competence. Based on all the available evidence, however, heroes seem to be conceptualized with a considerable amount of traditional breadth and depth, tempered at times with such shallow surface features as wealth, fame, and sexual attractiveness.

Klapp's (1962) five heroic types have a lot in common with the two main admirable characteristics identified by Csikszentmihalyi and Lyons (1982). Winners, splendid performers, and independent spirits (Klapp, 1962) seem to be admired for their personal competence (Csikszentmihalyi & Lyons, 1982); heroes of social acceptability and group servants (Klapp, 1962) seem closely allied with prosocial characteristics (Csikszentmihalyi & Lyons, 1982). Klapp (1962) and Csikszentmihalyi and Lyons differ, however, in their views of winning. Klapp has a separate category for winners, while the latter do not consider winning a separate, prominent attribute. Csikszentmihalyi and Lyons view winning as one of many personal competence characteristics.

In most studies dealing specifically with people's conceptions of highly praised athletes, exceptional playing skills are the most frequently admired characteristic. Csikszentmihalyi and Lyons would clearly label this characteristic personal competence. Furthermore, winning per se is not usually indentified as an independent attribute apart from athletic expertise. This parallels a similar lack of separate emphasis on winning in the work of Csikszentmihalyi and Lyons. Klapp's conceptualization of most athletes as splendid performers who do well in front of an audience suggests that consistently outstanding skill rather than merely winning is important. Much has been said about the importance attached by Americans to winning and being "number one." So far, however, the evidence concerning admiration of athletes points to broader veneration of their exceptional athletic talents, *not* specifically to their ability to win. Research designed to look more closely at this matter is probably warranted.

Smith (1973, 1976) developed an athletic hero typology based on later work by Klapp (1969) that outlines three categories: reinforcing, seductive, and transcendent. Smith believes that most sport heroes reinforce the societal status quo: They are highly skilled, show strong dedication to goals, demonstrate spectacular ability under pressure, come from behind to win, and often have individual charisma. He goes on to say that by the early 1970s a few seductive heroes had appeared; he names Muhammad Ali and Joe Namath as examples. A more recent illustration might be basketball player Charles Barkley, whose unconventional behavior on and off the court and tendency to speak his mind make him a media favorite. Seductive heroes are brash and arrogant, thumbing their noses at tradition but not going so far as to suggest attractive alternatives. Smith sees little evidence of transcendent athletic heroes—those who define enticing alternatives leading to social change.

Smith (1976) studied a wide age range of residents in Edmonton, Alberta, and his findings support his contention that reinforcing athletic heroes are the most prevalent. Respondents named a high proportion of these along with a few seductive heroes and no transcendent ones. Athletes identified as heroes were classified by Smith himself in one of these three categories. Whether respondents would have classified their heroes in similar ways is of course open to question. However, there is high agreement among respondents in Smith's study that excellent playing skill is the main quality that makes athletes heroic.

Vander Velden (1986) developed two categories of well-known athletes: heroes and bad winners. Athletic heroes are admired, and they portray important societal values and social relationships that tend to mirror the status quo. They are noted especially for their athletic ability and competitiveness. Bad winners are talented athletes who are nevertheless disliked for unsavory behavior, especially their arrogance and poor sportsmanship. He bases these categories on other scholars' and journalists' ideas and on college students' responses to a 1978 survey on their favorite and most disliked athletes. However, the students were asked about their likes and dislikes, not about heroes and bad winners. Vander Velden later applied these rubrics independently.

Although athletic heroes in Vander Velden's (1986) study were admired mainly for their athletic talent and competitiveness, several other qualities were also mentioned, albeit much less frequently: public image (all-American appeal, class), anti-individualism (unselfish, team-oriented), personality (nice, honest), self-confidence (confident, enthusiastic), intelligence (smart, creative), and appearance (handsome, good physique). Furthermore, bad winners were disliked in spite of their athletic excellence, primarily for their arrogance and poor sportsmanship and to a lesser extent for their bad public image, selfish individualism, and bad personality.

These data remind us that even though athletic talent is highly prominent, athletes are not held in high esteem for this single characteristic only. Other personal qualities are also recognized. In some cases these qualities may enhance traditionally heroic depth and breadth; in other cases personal qualities may be viewed as flaws that detract from greatness. Vander Velden's (1986) evidence shows that athletes are at times conceptualized by people in relatively traditional ways that contradict pessimistic charges of shallowness, whereas at other times they are perceived in ways that support pessimistic charges of flawed complexity. Respondents in Vander Velden's (1986) study did not identify athletes in the latter category as admirable or heroic, however. They distinguished between praiseworthy athletes and those undeserving of high esteem.

Vander Velden's (1986) work offers evidence that at least one star athlete has compartmentalized appeal. Muhammad Ali received the highest number of favorable *and* unfavorable responses. Clearly people disagreed considerably about Ali's praiseworthiness. In Vander Velden's (1986) terms, Ali was both a hero and a bad winner. His arrogance was the most salient negative characteristic. There is no indication of which respondents found him especially virtuous or especially reprehensible.

However, Vander Velden (1986) does point out several differences among the characteristics of heroes and bad winners identified by black and white students, again suggestive of compartmentalized appeal. Whites admired both athletic ability and competitiveness; blacks favored mainly athletic ability. Among the less frequently mentioned qualities, blacks admired physical appearance more than whites. Blacks found arrogance especially distasteful in athletes they disliked; whites also disliked arrogance, but disliked poor sportsmanship almost equally.

Other studies point to multifaceted conceptions of highly regarded athletes, supporting optimistic claims that they still retain traditionally heroic qualities. In a large survey of Americans covering a broad age range (Miller Brewing Company, 1983), respondents were given several preselected characteristics that they rated with regard to importance in choosing a favorite athlete. Athletic skill was judged highly important, but several other qualities had approximately equal value: personal conduct, moral character, personality, hard-hitting aggressiveness, and professionalism. Win/loss record and physical attractiveness were moderately important, whereas gender, race, and religion were less so. Furthermore, when American teenagers discussed reasons they held athletes in high regard, they coupled outstanding skills equally with dedication and hard work (Decision Research Corporation, 1984, p. 6).

The moderate importance given to physical attractiveness in one study suggests support for the pessimistic view emphasizing shallowness of athletic heroes. Physical attractiveness is clearly not a traditional heroic virtue. A question could also be raised about the heroic value of hard-hitting aggressiveness. This characteristic might be considered traditionally heroic if used to serve humanity (for example, saving someone from a mugger), but the evidence that people admire aggressiveness in athletes might support the pessimists' charges of flawed complexity. As it is, however, the evidence does not provide especially compelling support for the pessimists because it is not clear that respondents themselves considered aggressiveness a flaw and admired athletes in spite of it.

No other studies have produced evidence of people's high admiration of aggressiveness in athletes. Russell (1979) asked young Canadian male ice hockey players to identify their favorite players, and then performed his own independent assessment of two characteristics of those they chose, hockey skill (team statistics) and aggressiveness (penalties). Hockey skill was moderately associated with player popularity, but player popularity and aggressiveness showed no association. In Smith's (1976) study of residents of Edmonton, Alberta, aggressiveness was not reported as a reason for selection of athletic heroes. In the United States, surveys by Vander Velden (1986) and the Decision Research Corporation (1984) found no indication of admiration of aggressiveness in athletes. These findings must be countered, however, with more recent evidence that shows some people find violence in televised sport highly enjoyable (Bryant, 1989). More detailed study of people's admiration or condemnation of aggressiveness and violence in athletic heroes seems warranted.

We should note that Anderson (1979) found a greater tendency to identify a favorite team than a favorite player. Whole teams should perhaps be considered as admirable or heroic "characters," along with individual players. They are certainly more stable; players come and go yearly, whereas most teams stay put for decades. All studies indicate that athletic skills are of prime importance in people's admiration of teams (Russell, 1979; Smith, 1976; Miller Brewing Company, 1983), just as they are for admiration of individual players.

Numerous other less important but salient qualities are also thought to characterize praiseworthy teams, similar to individual players. However, the specific list seems to differ somewhat. For example, a modest relationship is shown between team popularity and *both* team aggressiveness and team hockey skills among young Canadian male ice hockey players' favorite teams (Russell, 1979). Previously we saw that only skills were salient for favorite individual players.

The large sample of Americans we have discussed was also asked to rate several preselected characteristics in importance as factors in leading them to root for a favorite team (Miller Brewing Company, 1983). Athletic skills were most important; familiarity with athletes, geographic location the team represents, past loyalty to the team, and coaching were moderately important. Least important were overall winning history, team administration, and race. Although these findings are interesting, they are not readily comparable with the admirable characteristics of respondents' favorite players because of differences in survey items.

To summarize, outstanding playing skills are clearly the most highly admired characteristic of praiseworthy athletes. This holds for players identified specifically as heroes as well as for all others. From the standpoint of Csikszentmihalyi and Lyons (1982) outstanding skill is a personal competence characteristic, which they would expect to be heavily admired in famous public figures—including star athletes. This finding is also congruent with Klapp's (1962) categorization of most athletes as splendid performers rather than winners; the focus is on the visible talents of athletes that delight and entertain the public. However, we should remember that athletes are admired for qualities beyond their playing skills, although these other qualities are less important. Somewhat robust, multifaceted characterizations are evident.

Returning to the debate about the ongoing existence of athletic heroes, the findings examined here so far are not particularly helpful. It is clear that praiseworthy athletes are perceived to have a moderate amount of depth and breadth of character, which partially supports optimistic contentions that athletes still have traditionally heroic qualities. In addition, athletic talent is an aspect of personal competence, and many would argue that personal competence is certainly a prominent feature of traditional heroism. This stance of course flies in the face of the pessimists' claims of shallowness. On the other hand, most of the breadth in characterizations is of secondary importance to the one-sided focus on athletic skills. Furthermore, there are hints of flawed complexity and compartmentalization. As we know, the optimists would evaluate these as indications of heroes' vitality, whereas the pessimists would judge them as evidence of heroes' collapse. In the case of flawed complexity, we can eliminate the problem of double-sided support by looking specifically at qualities judged as flaws by respondents in people whom they nevertheless consider heroic. For additional information about young people's characterizations of their athletic heroes, we turn now to the Greensboro study.

Hero Characterizations in the Greensboro Study

I grouped the characteristics used by the youths in the Greensboro study to describe their heroes into five categories: personal competence, social supportiveness, celebrity shallowness, negative, and miscellaneous. The first two—personal competence and social supportiveness—were developed from the work of Csikszentmihalyi and Lyons (1982). Personal competence involves an individual's own inherent excellence and mastery of valued skills. The Greensboro study showed two salient features: individual *expertise* (e.g., exceptional athletic skill, outstanding acting or musical talent, ability to lead a nation), and individual *ability to endure hardships* to reach goals (e.g., sustained hard work involving personal sacrifice to get to the top, risking one's life for a worthy cause, or the courage to live with chronic health problems).

Social supportiveness is centered on a positive inclination toward others. Termed "prosocial" by Csikszentmihalyi and Lyons (1982), characteristics in this category involve "the individual's willingness to invest his or her psychic energy for the well being of others'' (pp. 7-8). In the Greensboro study the most prominent aspects of this quality were *helpfulness to others* (nurturing children, saving lives, or serving others), possession of a *pleasant personality*, and having a *good sense of humor*.

The concept of celebrity shallowness grew out of the debate about the continued existence of heroes in contemporary American society. As we know, the pessimists take the position that heroes have disappeared, leaving behind a residue of hollow, shallow celebrities noted primarily for surface features such as fame, popularity, wealth, and good looks. The latter involves both bodily appearance and clothes. In Boorstin's (1961/1980) terms, such people are primarily ''notorious for their notoriety'' (p. 60). Entertainers and athletes are usually pointed out as prime examples.

In the Greensboro study the most prominent features of celebrity shallowness included *fame, physical appearance*, and *association with valued phenomena*. The first two qualities have obvious ties to the concept of shallowness developed by the pessimists, but the notion of association with valued phenomena needs further elaboration. Heroes were sometimes commended by respondents for their connection with activities that the respondents liked. Examples include playing on a favorite team, playing a favorite sport, or acting in a favorite television show or movie. Because mere association is not among traditional criteria for judging heroism, such association with valued phenomena is considered a manifestation of celebrity shallowness. We need to note, however, that in the interview respondents were asked to discuss ''famous heroes'' (see Appendix B), which might have either encouraged or discouraged inclusion of fame as part of their specific characterizations of the people they named. Interestingly, wealth was almost never mentioned.

The two other categories—negative characteristics and miscellaneous characteristics—were developed to encompass the remainder of the youths' comments about their heroes. Few respondents gave unfavorable, negative characterizations. The interview format progressed from a discussion of admirable people to a discussion of heroes, which likely steered respondents away from identifying negative qualities. Furthermore, no specific request for information about negative qualities was made in the interview. Thus negative characteristics may have been underreported.

I tried to classify as negative only those perceptions considered negative by the youths themselves, but this was sometimes difficult. In some rare cases a respondent characterized a hero in a negative way, recognized the perception as negative, and said that nevertheless this negative quality was appealing about the person. In other cases a respondent looked up to a hero in spite of recognizing certain negative characteristics as flaws. And in some cases respondents' characterizations appeared to be negative, but nothing clearly indicated that they thought their perceptions were negative.

Although hampered somewhat by these ambiguities, the category of negative characteristics contains qualities judged by the author to be perceived unfavorably by the youths themselves. Few negative characteristics were mentioned, and because they were not particularly salient their analytical usefulness is somewhat limited. They have occasional relevance to the debate, however, as they can be used to address the concern about flawed complexity—because they are confined to qualities perceived negatively by respondents themselves. People thinking their heroes have negative qualities and identifying them as heroes anyway constitutes fairly strong evidence for the existence of flawed complexity in heroes.

Main themes in the negative comments are primarily ''opposites'' of personal competence, social supportiveness, and celebrity shallowness. Remember that on the positive side, respondents considered all three of these qualities praiseworthy. Some youths mentioned unpleasant personality qualities such as a bad temper, excessive violence, meanness, and selfishness. Others said that having outstanding competence in specialized areas like acting, athletics, or music was not enough to make a person heroic. Some also saw a comparatively low level of expertise in a particular hero as detrimental to praiseworthiness. Others commented on lack of physical appeal. Finally, a number of youths thought that people formerly noted for greatness but no longer in the limelight were less praiseworthy than those still in the public eye.

As suggested by the name of the category, miscellaneous characteristics consisted of a variety of qualities difficult to classify. Although some appear to fit easily into one of the other categories, they were discussed by the respondents in ways that made such correspondence difficult. A few of the miscellaneous comments involved a particular hero's possession of specific demographic characteristics (e.g., gender, race, age) that were seen as attractive. Occasionally someone suggested that being the nation's president was in itself sufficient for praiseworthiness, regardless of the person's activities while in office.

The three main sets of characteristics—personal competence, social supportiveness, and celebrity shallowness—are our central focus. Examining these comparatively can shed light on the extent to which the young people conceptualized their athletic heroes as shallow celebrities or as more traditionally substantive heroes possessing personal competence and social supportiveness. In addition, negative characterizations occasionally provide evidence of flawed complexity. Finally, evidence of compartmentalized appeal occurs occasionally in the form of gender and race differences in the youths' characterizations. Disagreements among various groups of respondents about whether particular qualities are flaws or positive characteristics might also suggest compartmentalization, but these are not evident in the Greensboro data.

In what follows we will first compare and contrast the Greensboro youths' characterizations of famous, well-known athletic heroes with their perceptions of famous heroes from other walks of life. Then we will explore their views of athletic heroes who are personal acquaintances, comparing these with the famous, public figures.

Data are insufficient to warrant a major section addressing comparisons based on gender, race, and grade level. Because there was little previous work on this topic, we wanted to carry out such analyses in the Greensboro study. In many cases, however, when one of these demographic variables was introduced the number of comments by particular groups of respondents about particular groups of heroes became too small to be meaningful. This was especially problematic for the grade level analyses because there were four grades in the Greensboro study. Several interesting pieces of comparative information were obtained from the gender and race analyses, however, and these are included in appropriate subsections below.

Well-Known Athletes Compared With Other Famous People

Selection frequencies show that most athletic heroes are famous public figures. It is useful then to examine the ways that young people conceive of them in comparison with well-known people from other walks of life. In the Greensboro study the most frequently mentioned others were entertainers and political or military leaders. Quantitative data consist of the frequencies with which heroes were described using particular characteristics, categorized as personal competence, social supportiveness, celebrity shallowness, negative, and miscellaneous. Qualitative data consist of the youths' conceptions of the two most frequently chosen athletes (Tony Dorsett and Reggie Jackson), entertainers (Burt Reynolds and Diana Ross), and political or military leaders (Ronald Reagan and Martin Luther King, Jr.). These provide detailed illustrations of the main findings in the quantitative data, including direct quotes from the interview transcriptions. The primary focus in both analyses is on the extent to which and the ways in which shallowness and traditional heroism were salient in the young people's conceptions of the athletes they identified as heroic. Scattered findings of flawed complexity and compartmentalization are also noted.

Frequencies of Hero Characterizations: Quantitative Analysis

The quantitative data are presented as percentages of the youths' comments falling within each of the main categories of characteristics previously outlined—personal competence, social supportiveness, celebrity shallowness, negative, and miscellaneous. These are displayed in bar graphs (for example, see Figure 3.1). On each graph percentages at the top of the bars refer to proportions of the total number of characteristics included *in that graph*. These percentages total 100%, with minor discrepancies due to rounding errors. The total number of comments on which each graph is based is also noted, along with the total number of heroes. In most cases the number of heroes is larger than the number of comments because respondents often chose not to discuss the characteristics of every hero they named.

Recall that a small number of heroes classified as athletes, entertainers, and political or military leaders were involved in these respective fields in other ways (e.g., coaches, sportscasters, models, authors, staff members to politicians). But because these others are small in number, heroes in each group are often referred to collectively using the main rubric identifying the majority of people in a category. First we will examine the youths' characterizations of athletes; then we will compare these with their views of entertainers and political or military leaders.

Famous Athletes

Quantitative data concerning well-known athletes come from the youths' responses in two different sections of the interview (see Appendix A and Appendix B). Early on, they were asked to discuss their broad collection of heroes (including athletes), and later they were asked specifically about athletes. In both sets of questioning, publicly known athletes were clearly praised for their personal competence; over 40% of the comments referred to this quality (see Figures 3.1 and 3.2). Most of the remarks concerned outstanding athletic skills, mixed with ability to win. A considerably smaller number dealt with endurance of hardships such as long years of hard practice, poverty or other inhospitable circumstances, and the pain and violence of intense competition.

Famous athletes were also occasionally characterized as socially supportive. Comparatively, however, these comments totaled less than a third of those dealing with personal competence. Athletes' social supportiveness was usually connected directly to sport and concerned attention to teamwork and ability to help a team achieve victory. Heroic star athletes were not often noted for other aspects of social supportiveness such as aid to others in need, pleasant personality, or sense of humor.

Celebrity shallowness was also occasionally used to characterize well-known athletes, but again these comments totaled only about one third of those relevant

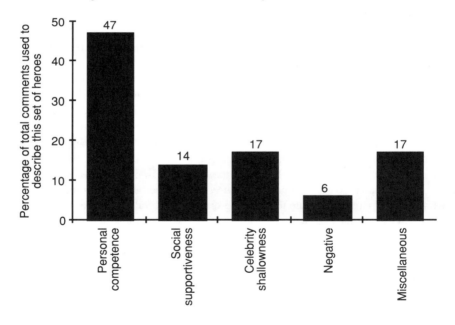

Figure 3.1.   Characterizations of famous athletic heroes from sport-only questioning. Number of respondents = 128; frequency of comments = 102; frequency of heroes = 382.

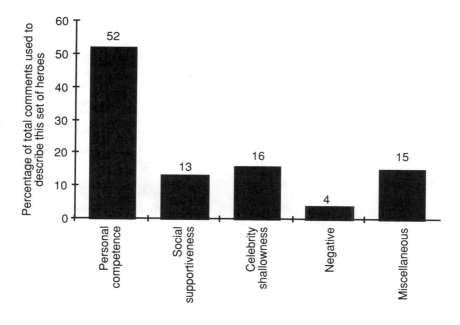

Figure 3.2.   Characterizations of famous athletic heroes from all-walks-of-life questioning. Data are from the general section of the interview. Number of respondents = 128; frequency of comments = 48; frequency of heroes = 133.

to personal competence. Most comments focused on association with valued phenomena, such as being on a respondent's favorite team or having exceptional talent in a respondent's favorite sport. Quite a few also dealt with the high public visibility—fame—of heroic athletes. Physical appearance is clearly a central feature of celebrity shallowness, but the youths made no comments about this characteristic in connection with famous heroic athletes.

Remarks about negative characteristics of well-known athletes accounted for less than 10% of the total. They included observations of temper tantrums, evaluations of some people as less athletically talented than others, and indications that some athletes had passed their prime competitively. In addition, occasionally some noted that sport is not as important as things other heroes do, such as working for greater social justice or using one's expertise to help ordinary people. Most of these observations seem indicative of flawed complexity. Perceptions of low importance of sport perhaps imply celebrity shallowness: Athletes were rebuked for their narrow focus on sport, which some thought to be a limitation on heroic greatness.

Overall, well-known athletic heroes were distinguished primarily for personal competence centered in athletic expertise. Social supportiveness was much less salient, as was celebrity shallowness. Negative characteristics were even less prominent.

I identified an interesting race comparison in the youths' conceptions of famous athletes (see Figure 3.3). The black respondents placed relatively equal emphasis on personal competence and social supportiveness of white athletes, but for black athletes they followed the familiar pattern of strong, singular emphasis on personal competence. On the other hand, the white respondents carried out the familiar pattern of major emphasis on personal competence for both black and white athletes. The divergence may be because black youths' conceptions of white athletes are based on only 11 comments. With such a small number, addition or deletion of only a few remarks would greatly change these percentages. We will see shortly, however, that this finding might be part of a larger trend.

Gender analyses yielded less interesting comparative information. Overall, the boys' and girls' conceptions were similar and thus obviously paralleled what we have already seen for the sample as a whole. The girls selected quite a few famous female athletes as heroes, but the boys selected none—which made it impossible to compare characterizations simultaneously on the basis of gender of respondents and gender of heroes.

Famous Entertainers

Personal competence, social supportiveness, and celebrity shallowness were cited with about equal frequency in characterizations of well-known entertainers as heroes (see Figure 3.4). About one fourth of the comments fell into each of these categories. This relative evenness may be because heroes from several distinct areas of endeavor were combined (musicians, singers, dancers, television and movie actors, cartoon characters, characters from literary works, and authors). In addition, entertainment may permit greater flexibility of action and make it possible to demonstrate a wider variety of characteristics.

Personal competence was tied mainly to entertainment talents—dramatic and musical expertise figured prominently. Also occasionally noted was the ability of movie and television characters to endure hardships in the course of saving people or reaching other goals.

Respondents focused heavily on social supportiveness for characters in television shows and movies, praising these characters' helpfulness to people in distress, often risking their own lives in the process. A few comedians and cartoon characters were commended for being light-hearted and funny, but this occurred relatively infrequently. A pleasant personality and being easy to get along with are important components of social supportiveness, but these were almost never mentioned in characterizations of the entertainers.

The fame of well-known entertainers was the most salient aspect of their shallowness. Many respondents thought that extensive public acclaim contributed to heroic greatness. Occasional note was also made of a hero's association with valued phenomena such as a particular movie, television show, or type of music. Physical appearance was mentioned, but rather infrequently. With the high visibility of attractiveness and trendy clothes among entertainers, the lack of emphasis on physical appearance is especially noteworthy. Perhaps respondents held back

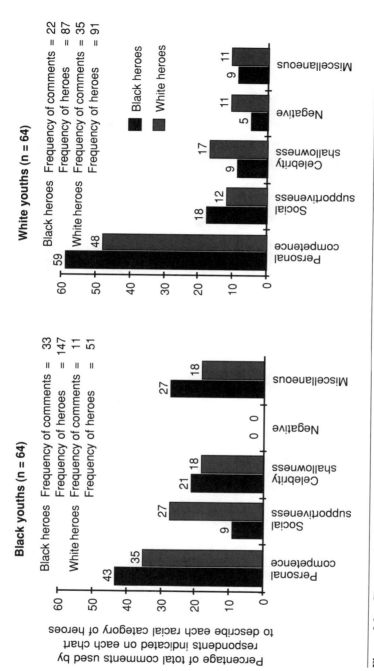

Figure 3.3. **Characterizations of famous athletic heroes of black and white respondents, by race of heroes.** Data are from the sport section of the interview. Data for a small percentage of heroes not classified as black or white have been omitted. Note the differences in the frequencies of comments about black and white heroes compared on each chart.

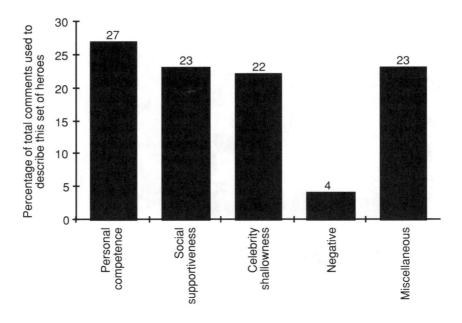

Figure 3.4.   Characterizations of famous entertainment heroes from all-walks-of-life questioning. Data are from the general section of the interview. Number of respondents = 128; frequency of comments = 134; frequency of heroes = 225.

some of their admiration for these qualities so as not to appear shallow to the adult interviewers. On the other hand, perhaps they genuinely did not consider these qualities particularly heroic.

Remarks about negative characteristics of publicly known entertainers were uncommon, accounting for less than 5% of the total. Movie and television characters were occasionally condemned for wanting to fight too much or being too slick. Some said that fictional characters would be more heroic if they were real. The musical or dramatic talents of several entertainers were thought to be less than exceptional. Occasionally a respondent commented negatively about the type of music produced by a particular person. Flawed complexity is suggested by many of the comments, while celebrity shallowness is elicited by the observation that fictional status implies some amount of insignificance.

Overall, heroic, well-known entertainers were characterized about equally often for personal competence (centered primarily on entertainment talents), social supportiveness (focused mainly on helpfulness of movie and television characters), and celebrity shallowness (primarily emphasizing fame and association with particular television shows, movies, and music liked by respondents).

Famous Political or Military Leaders

Over 50% of the comments about well-known political or military leaders focused on social supportiveness (see Figure 3.5). Emphasis was placed on helping the

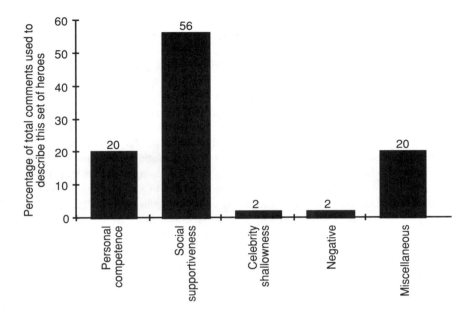

Figure 3.5.   Characterizations of famous political and military heroes from all-walks-of-life questioning. Data are from the general section of the interview. Number of respondents = 128; frequency of comments = 103; frequency of heroes = 92.

country achieve major political and social objectives such as succeeding against other world powers, generally staying on course, and advancing domestic social change movements such as civil rights. Having an easygoing, pleasant personality is an important component of social supportiveness, but this was almost never mentioned in connection with these national and international leaders.

Personal competence appeared in 20% of the remarks about famous political or military figures. They were most often praised for their willingness and ability to endure hardships associated with steadfastness in their ideals—at times risking their lives, or even dying—to chart the global future of the nation or to work for social justice on the domestic front. Their general political or military expertise was also occasionally noted.

Overall, well-known political or military heroes were commended most for their social supportiveness (centered on helping the nation), and secondarily for their personal competence (focused on enduring the hardships of accomplishing major political and military goals). There were almost no remarks about negative characteristics or celebrity shallowness.

Gender and Race Comparisons
I could not make gender and race comparisons among famous athletes, entertainers, and political or military leaders because the number of comments pertaining

to any one group was too small to be meaningful. Instead comparisons were made using the youths' responses to questions about their broad collection of famous heroes from all walks of life (see Appendix B). The proportions of athletes, entertainers, political or military leaders, and others in this group are displayed in Figure 2.1 (see page 35).

We will look first at race comparisons (see Figure 3.6). The black youths emphasized personal competence and social supportiveness about equally in descriptions of their black heroes, whereas they focused more strongly on the social supportiveness of their white heroes. The white youths, on the other hand, placed about equal importance on personal competence and social supportiveness of their white heroes, whereas they stressed personal competence of their black heroes. Both groups of respondents attended equally to the two characteristics in same-race heroes, and then stressed one or the other in opposite-race heroes.

This full pattern did not exist in the youths' conceptions of famous athletes, as previously examined (see Figure 3.3). One similarity between the two analyses, however, was a tendency for the black youths to emphasize social supportiveness in white heroes more than the white youths did, and a tendency for the white youths to emphasize personal competence in black heroes more than the black youths did.

Perhaps the black youths believed that the dominant positions occupied by white heroes in American society enable them to help people in need. If so, this conception may have carried over to athletics as well. On the other hand, the white youths may have had fewer opportunities to observe blacks engaging in socially supportive behavior, which may have contributed to their heavier focus on the personal competence of black heroes. We also should remember that a large majority of the famous black heroes named by the white respondents were athletes, and we saw earlier that athletes were heavily praised for their personal competence. Similarly, entertainers comprised a majority of the black youths' white heroes, and we know that entertainers were commended somewhat more equally for personal competence and social supportiveness. These circumstances contributed to the overall greater attention given by the black youths to social supportiveness in white heroes.

The relatively equal emphasis on personal competence and social supportiveness of famous same-race heroes from all walks of life may have been due to the youths' greater familiarity with members of their own race. As a result, they may have been aware of a wider set of qualities that characterize same-race heroes. Furthermore, the relatively equal distribution of same-race heroes among athletes, entertainers, and political or military leaders may have contributed to more balanced characterizations. It cannot easily be explained why this pattern did not carry over to same-race athletic heroes. Perhaps the prominence of personal competence was so strong for athletes that it overrode the potential for greater balance rooted in same-race familiarity.

These findings suggest somewhat compartmentalized conceptions of famous heroes in general, and famous athletic heroes in particular. In terms of the debate about the continued existence of athletic heroes, we should remember

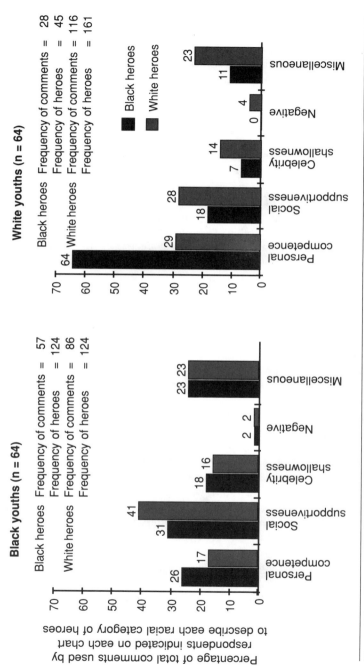

Figure 3.6. Characterizations of black and white respondents' famous heroes from all walks of life, by race of heroes. Data are from the general section of the interview. Data for a small percentage of heroes not classified as black or white have been omitted. Note the differences in the frequencies of comments about black and white heroes compared on each chart.

that compartmentalization can be viewed optimistically as a sign of cultural vitality or pessimistically as a sign of loss of shared values. The mere presence of compartmentalization may serve mainly to fuel the controversy.

We noted earlier the possibility that racial stereotyping may underlie differences in hero choice patterns. Recall that the white youths selected a preponderance of athletes among their black heroes, whereas the black youths selected a large number of entertainers among their white heroes. However, racial stereotyping was not evident in the young people's hero characterizations. Differences existed, as we have just seen, but these do not seem linked specifically to traditional American racial stereotypes. However, the high proportion of athletes among the white youths' black heroes, coupled with frequent commendations of the physical skills of all athletes, makes it important to keep racial stereotyping in mind here. Further study of this topic seems warranted.

Gender comparisons using the same combination of athletes, entertainers, political or military leaders, and others (see Figure 2.1, page 35) also yielded an interesting finding (see Figure 3.7). The girls characterized this broad set of famous heroes with somewhat greater emphasis on social supportiveness, whereas the boys focused a little more on personal competence. This difference gives a hint of compartmentalized appeal.

The girls' emphasis on social supportiveness among their broad group of heroes was contrary to their conceptions of famous athletes. We learned earlier that both the boys and girls used the familiar pattern of primary emphasis on personal competence coupled with secondary focus on social supportiveness and celebrity shallowness to characterize well-known athletic heroes. Athletes were perceived in similar ways by the boys and girls, but the girls chose fewer of them than the boys did.

Much evidence indicates that females in American society are more oriented than males toward nurturing and interpersonal support (Huston, 1983), undoubtedly because of traditional domestic and child-rearing responsibilities of females. So the girls' greater emphasis on social supportiveness in their famous heroes comes as no surprise. On the other hand, males are more oriented toward dominance and independence (Huston, 1983), which is likely at the root of the boys' heavier emphasis on personal competence. Furthermore, the girls selected fewer athletes and more entertainers and political or military leaders among their broad set of heroes. Compared to athletes, we know that both of these other groups were more strongly characterized as socially supportive, which perhaps also contributed to the girls' greater focus on social supportiveness.

Most Frequently Selected Athletes, Entertainers, and Political or Military Leaders: Qualitative Analysis

The Greensboro youths' conceptualizations of famous heroes can be examined in greater detail by considering their comments about particular people. I analyzed the two most frequently mentioned athletes (Tony Dorsett and Reggie Jackson), entertainers (Burt Reynolds and Diana Ross), and political or military leaders (Ronald Reagan and Martin Luther King, Jr.). To give this a somewhat broader

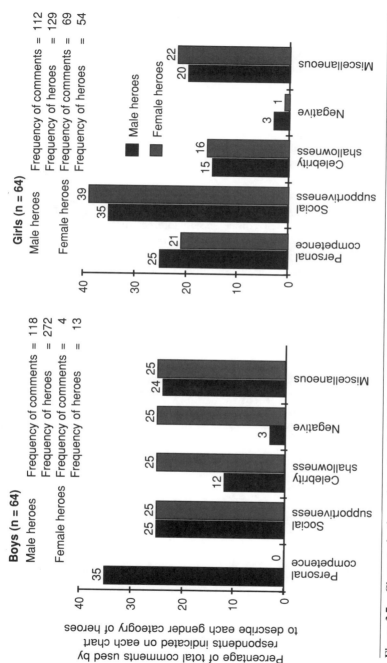

Figure 3.7. **Characterizations of boys' and girls' famous heroes from all walks of life, by gender of heroes.** Data are from the general section of the interview. Data for a small percentage of heroes not classified as male or female have been omitted. Note the differences in the frequencies of comments about male and female heroes compared on each chart.

context, Tables 2.4, 2.5, and 2.6 list respondents' top 10 choices of athletes, entertainers, and political or military leaders.

The interviews consisted of discussions of admirable people, followed by considerations of heroes (see Appendix A and Appendix B). Differences in the nature of the data obtained from the two types of questioning were minimal. In carrying out the qualitative analyses, therefore, I combined comments referring to admirable people and heroes. In the case of the two athletes, data from both the general and sport-specific sections of the interview were used. Quotations from the interview data support the findings summarized here, and help to illustrate the quantitative evidence already presented.

Top Two Athletes: Tony Dorsett and Reggie Jackson

Clearly, the primary reason Tony Dorsett and Reggie Jackson were considered heroic was outstanding personal competence, centered in their athletic skills. This is in line with the quantitative data already discussed. In looking at the details of the nature of outstanding skills for Dorsett and Jackson, however, we learn that conceptualizations of the two differed. Not surprisingly, former Dallas Cowboys running back Tony Dorsett was admired especially for his running ability, and former California Angels outfielder Reggie Jackson was noted primarily for his batting skill.

Dorsett was characterized as a fast runner who went through rough spots without the need for blocking, who never messed up, who made the most points on his team, and who was acclaimed for his great deeds by being named Most Valuable Player. Furthermore, he was thought to have worked hard to achieve his boyhood goal of becoming a professional football player, and he courageously endured the pain that comes from playing football. Quotes from respondents illustrate their characterizations:

> *He wanted to be a running back, and he always wanted to be on the Dallas Cowboys, and he got drafted, and that's what he wanted.*
> *He can run very fast, and he got the moves that hardly no other football player got.*
> *He can run faster than Mean Joe Green.*
> *I like his moves, or the way he moves.*
> *He quick in faking.*
> *He goes through the rough spots, and if there ain't no blocking, he goes.*
> *They [Tony Dorsett and Ron Springs] can make in football the most points and the most touchdowns, and most valuable player, and they never mess up.*
> *They [Tony Dorsett and others] got to take hits, and they got to take when people be clipping them and pushing them down.*

Jackson was portrayed as a good baseball player who hit a lot of home runs and other long balls, making him one of the top competitors in his field. Examples of comments include the following:

He can hit the ball far.
He's a powerful hitter in baseball.
He can hit a ball harder than I ever known, and he can run very fast.
He's a good hitter.
He always hits home runs.
I just like to see him hit his home runs.
I admire . . . just the performance in his game, being one of the top competitors. Being good in his field.

Dorsett was also viewed to be socially supportive, although this was much less salient than his personal athletic competence. It was said that he possessed good sportsmanship, helped his team win, and took the time to help youngsters learn the game. Social supportiveness was not used to characterize Jackson. Comments about Dorsett include these:

I respect his great football, team spirit.
He helps children. . . . He teaches children what he knows.
He has good sportsmanship toward the other members.
Everybody be lookin' for him to . . . make the touchdowns and stuff like that.
He can play football real good and throw a pass, intercept the balls and make points for the team, and make the team happy.

Celebrity shallowness was also used occasionally to characterize both players, but relatively infrequently. Both were thought to be praiseworthy because of their affiliations with favorite teams—the Dallas Cowboys or the New York Yankees (Jackson's team before he joined the Angels in 1982). Good looks and fame were mentioned as reasons for holding both of them in high regard, and both were also thought to be praiseworthy merely for being in television commercials. Respondents made comments like these about Dorsett:

He's a famous running back for the Dallas Cowboys.
He was my favorite. Dallas is my favorite team.
Tony Dorsett's on that Hi-C commercial.
People like him a lot. They brag about him, so I gotta go along with 'em.
He been around a long time. He's pretty popular.
He's cute.
Sort of a celebrity type guy. He gets on all the Coke commercials and stuff.

Similar comments were also made about Jackson:

I admire his pitches, his team spirit, good commercials.
Lots of people know him.
He's a famous . . . Yankee. That's why I like him.
He's on my favorite team.
Reggie, he's famous. . . . He is more talked about on TV.

Negative characteristics were used occasionally to describe Jackson, but not Dorsett. Jackson was characterized as possessing a mean streak that at times led him to get into fights with other players and to engage in other kinds of unsportsmanlike behavior. He was also acknowledged to be a less than complete ballplayer, though his exceptional batting talent was viewed as almost compensatory for his poor play on the field. The negative characteristics are illustrated by these comments:

> *Sometimes when Reggie Jackson has three strikes in a row and he yells at the pitcher sometimes.*
> *He wouldn't usually get in a fight with the referee or nothing like that. He probably kick some dust on him or something, but he wouldn't hit him.*
> *I don't think he has good sportsmanship.*
> *He's terrible on the field, and all he can do is hit.*
> *He's kinda mean.*

These negative characterizations support the notion of flawed complexity. Jackson's baseball talent was acknowledged; it was the main source of his admiration and heroism. Nevertheless he was viewed by some of his admirers as somewhat less than perfect. The Greensboro youths were not the only ones to notice Jackson's negative qualities. He appeared second behind Muhammad Ali on a list of bad winners named by a group of college students in 1978 (Vander Velden, 1986).

Both Dorsett and Jackson were praised most often for their personal competence—their athletic talent. At first glance this rather unidimensional, flat conception might be considered evidence of celebrity shallowness. Both lacked depth and breadth of character in the eyes of the Greensboro youths, which would support the pessimistic position in the debate about the ongoing existence of athletic heroes. Jackson's flawed complexity provides additional backing for the pessimists. We should remember, however, that personal competence is a traditionally heroic characteristic. The performance of great deeds requiring extraordinary talent is clearly a mainstay of the idealized, archetypical conception of the hero. In addition, Dorsett's personal competence was somewhat more broadly conceived, and he was occasionally commended for his social supportiveness—which buttresses the optimists' position in the debate.

Top Two Entertainers: Burt Reynolds and Diana Ross

The youths' characterizations of Burt Reynolds and Diana Ross focused on personal competence, which was almost always defined by their exceptional entertainment skills. Ross was viewed as a good singer, but a number of youths emphasized her multifaceted talents extending to dancing and acting as well:

> *She sings well.*
> *Her singing is real good.*
> *She's a famous singer, movie star.*
> *She sings, she dances, she acts. She a well-rounded, very talented person.*

Reynolds was viewed as a talented actor; beyond this, the talents of the characters he played were also sometimes praised. Examples included physical stunts (many of which he was thought to do himself), ability to outrun policemen in catching enemies, ability to handle trouble, and ability to attract women. The following quotes illustrate what the respondents thought of Reynolds:

> *He be in a lot of movies. He makes very good shows.*
> *He's about the best actor.*
> *I . . . like the stunts that he played in, when I watched "Smokey and the Bandit." I think he has a lot of courage to wanna jump over things like that.*
> *He has his own stunts. He does his own, most of them.*
> *Richard Pryor and Burt Reynolds, they can run from each other and they . . . can outrun policemen, and catch enemies for nobody else wouldn't be able to get killed.*
> *In all the movies he played in he always has a lady.*
> *They [Jane Fonda and Burt Reynolds] always seem to . . . play themselves in the movies, things that they would do in real life.*

Reynolds' characters also were occasionally commended for social support-iveness, though infrequently. Championing good over evil is one example. Reynolds himself was also admired for occasionally being funny and lighthearted and having a good personality:

> *He seems like a nice person, fun to get along with.*
> *He likes to do a lot of crazy stuff. . . . In his movies he's really funny.*
> *He's always the good guy, and . . . sometimes he's funny in movies.*
> *He's funnier . . . and he can make me laugh and everything.*

Celebrity shallowness was clearly evident in the characterizations of the two entertainers. Both were viewed as famous and wealthy, and Reynolds was also considered good-looking. Ross was viewed as praiseworthy partly because the songs she sang were liked by respondents, and Reynolds was commended partly because he played in good movies. Celebrity qualities were not of central importance in the youths' perceptions of these two entertainers, but they were definitely present. No comments were made about negative characteristics of either Ross or Reynolds. Here are some examples of quotes showing Reynolds' celebrity shallowness:

> *He's famous. He's cute.*
> *He makes a lot of movies, and he makes good money and stuff, and a lot of people like him, like to watch his shows.*
> *He's made a name for himself, and everybody knows who Burt Reynolds is.*
> *He's good-looking.*
> *I like going to see funny movies.*
> *He's just famous. I like him a whole lot.*

The following comments illustrate Ross's celebrity shallowness:

She sings real good, she wears good clothes, and I like her looks.
I like to sing a lot, and I like to listen to records. I like Diana Ross.
She's famous.
Her songs are good.
She's really famous.
She's made it. . . . That's what makes her, I guess.

Neither Reynolds nor Ross were conceptualized with equal emphasis on personal competence, social supportiveness, and celebrity shallowness. Both of their portrayals diverged somewhat from the equality across these three characteristics found in the previous quantitative data. Reynolds was described with greater breadth than Ross, so he came closer to typifying the quantitative data. Celebrity shallowness was somewhat salient for both, which supports the pessimistic position in the debate. Nevertheless, there was much greater emphasis on personal competence of both (albeit a somewhat unidimensional emphasis on entertainment talents, especially for Ross), and secondary attention to social supportiveness for Reynolds. This focus on traditionally heroic qualities supports the optimistic position.

Top Two Political or Military Leaders: Ronald Reagan and Martin Luther King, Jr.

Comments about Ronald Reagan and Martin Luther King, Jr., show that social supportiveness was the most salient feature of both, and personal competence also figured prominently. Celebrity shallowness was not viewed as important for either man, which is congruent with our previous quantitative data.

Social supportiveness was the most frequently mentioned and broadly defined characteristic. Martin Luther King, Jr., was portrayed as helpful in improving American society, employing nonviolent protest toward achieving equality. Here are some of the comments on King:

He helped black people.
Martin Luther King was the type of man that like to see people together; working together, living together.
If it hadn't been for him, so many people wouldn't be . . . together in the world today.
He stood for people uniting. That made him famous, his fight uniting his people.
He stood up for his rights to make black people free.
He stood up for his rights, and . . . the way he didn't use violence. Instead he went on marches and preached, and he didn't believe in any violence.
He was fighting for the blacks, and they look up to him 'cause he fought for us.
He helped us to see about blacks and whites and the difference between them and us, and that we shouldn't be different.

He tried to get the black people from out of slavery, and he had a dream.
Martin Luther King did a lot to change things. . . . The KKK and everything.
He helped to stop that.

Ronald Reagan was president when the Greensboro study was conducted. People thought he was doing as much as he could to help the country overcome its economic woes and to maintain national security in the face of international threat. These are some of the comments from respondents:

He's doing a tremendous job in office.
Right now he's getting pretty famous with his budget cuts and everything
that he's been doin', and I think he's just trying to get this country into
a better economic situation.
He's tried so hard to try and get this country back . . . so people can buy
things nowadays.
He is trying to help the people.
He's helping the country as much as he can.
His ability to lead . . . and what he knows.
He's got the guts to be president and try to fix things.
Reagan, for stepping in at these times, especially the time the world's in
right now, how hard it is and everything. And how he's taking control
and taking the cutbacks and everything and trying to make money more
of what it was before the depression or whatever.

Personal competence was closely tied to social supportiveness. King's personal competence included enduring hardships brought on by his desire and efforts to effect social change. Also mentioned was his eventual assassination.

His assassination . . . . That's what made him. I mean, it was a tragic ac-
cident.
He did die for his cause, that's the reason why he was killed. He was
fighting very hard to win freedom for everyone. He died in the process.
He always kept his spirits up, besides what was taking place outside. . . .
No matter how bad odds were or what was going on, just all the violence,
he never would fight back and just loved his enemies.
King has just so many things going against him. Just every corner he
turned there were just something that would take place. He had to sit
in jail, and he was hit with sticks, he just had to turn every cheek.

Reagan was commended for his endurance of the stressful hardships of being president, including the assassination attempt that occurred shortly after he took office. These are comments about the hardships he weathered:

He's old yet he's . . . in office right now. He's not worried about, well,
maybe if I do this, next election time they won't . . . elect me into office
or whatever. He says I'm gonna do what's right. . . . Being shot and
all that, . . . he's just really great.

Lookin' back on the assassination, I think that was, a lot of people admired
   him for his strength through that.
The way he handled the assassination.

Along with the many similarities between the youths' images of King and
Reagan, there were also differences—primarily due to negative characterizations
of Reagan not used with King. Perhaps this difference is partly explained by the
relative immediacy of the two men's activities: Reagan was alive and active,
whereas King was a historical figure no longer living. The stormy history of
American race relations and the centrality of the position of an elected president
make the doubt about Reagan and positive unanimity about King almost paradoxi-
cal. In spite of occasional negative comments, the young people who identified
Reagan as praiseworthy included 73% whites and 27% blacks. Those who held
King in high regard included 21% whites and 79% blacks. By some, Reagan
was portrayed as an unfair president whose policies selectively helped particular
Americans more than others. Furthermore, Reagan was given almost grudging,
knee-jerk praise in some cases because he occupied the office of President of
the United States, which in itself was sufficient reason to hold him in high regard.
Of course not all youths who named Reagan as a hero mentioned negative points,
but he did receive his share, as the following comments illustrate:

He's not helping people, he's not out to help people, he's out to help
   his people.
He became president, so that got him to be famous.
He's the president. What can you say to that?
Why doesn't he use his money instead of the taxpayers'?
He is going to start another war one day.

The negative characteristics used to describe Reagan provide clear evidence
of flawed complexity. In spite of considering him admirable or heroic, some
young people noted significant blemishes, which lends support to the pessimistic
position in the debate. However, there was little celebrity shallowness in the
youths' conceptualizations of either man, and both were considered strong in
social supportiveness and personal competence, which favors the optimists.

Summary and Implications: Well-Known Athletes Compared
With Other Famous Heroes

The quantitative data provide broad perspectives on the Greensboro youths'
conceptualizations of famous heroes, while the qualitative data give us greater
depth of knowledge about a few particular people. The two are considerably
congruent. Athletes were most frequently praised for their personal competence;
political or military leaders were most often commended for their social supportiveness; and entertainers were held in high regard almost equally for their personal
competence, social supportiveness, and celebrity shallowness.

The prominence of praise for the personal competence of famous athletes
parallels the findings of several earlier studies. Results of this earlier work indicate

that athletic talent was highly admired (Decision Research Corporation, 1984; Miller Brewing Company, 1983; Russell, 1979; Smith, 1976; Vander Velden, 1986), at times in conjunction with other characteristics (Decision Research Corporation, 1984; Miller Brewing Company, 1983; Vander Velden, 1986). In the Greensboro study modest attention was also given to other characteristics of famous athletic heroes—social supportiveness and celebrity shallowness. However, neither of these was especially prominent.

It has been observed that mass media portrayals of sporting events tend to trivialize athletic skills (Chalip & Chalip, 1989; Hughes & Coakley, 1984). Other studies show that athletic skills are a major focus of media coverage (Harris & Hills, 1993; Hilliard, 1984). These latter studies, however, do not examine the breadth and detail with which athletic talents are presented. Part of the trivialization involves rather undetailed yet glamorous accounts. Spectacular plays are noted, but without much commentary on complicated technical and experiential aspects. If the mass media are downplaying athletic talents, it does not seem to show in young people's conceptualizations of athletic heroes. They still admire athletes mainly for their playing skills. Little is known, however, about the amount of technical sophistication young people use to characterize and evaluate such talents. More work in the area seems warranted.

Contrary to evidence from Csikszentmihalyi and Lyons (1982) demonstrating that public figures from all walks of life were admired most often for their personal competence, the results of the Greensboro study show a greater variety of characterizations. Perceptions of famous athletic heroes had the greatest similarity to the Csikszentmihalyi and Lyons results. In addition, little evidence suggested a conceptual split in the minds of the respondents between athletic talent and ability to win games, which supports the more all-encompassing model developed by Csikszentmihalyi and Lyons rather than Klapp's (1962) earlier view in which the two are clearly separated.

The skills of outstanding athletes are constantly on public display. Furthermore, these skills are analyzed in graphic detail on television with the aid of slow-motion and instant replay. Although political or military leaders are constantly seen on television, the specific skills they possess have not usually been analyzed with as much precision (although this may be changing somewhat in the early 1990s, as seen in the increased sophistication of television coverage of the technical aspects of the Gulf War). Entertainers' talents are also constantly in front of the public eye, but they are not analyzed and dissected as extensively as those of athletes. The different amounts of attention given to personal competence of these three groups may depend on the salience with which public examination of their skills is included in media presentations. In cases where personal competence is not examined in much detail, this characteristic may remain abstract and nebulous in people's minds.

In contrast to political or military leaders, athletes were not often cited for their social supportiveness. Athletes also received less praise for this quality than entertainers did. Although helping one's team achieve victory was occasionally salient, it remains clear that athletes were not often seen to display broad-based social supportiveness. Political or military leaders frequently deal with situations in which their support can affect many people. Actors, by virtue of the endless variety of roles they play, may have the potential to create broader, more complex images involving greater amounts of social supportiveness. We should also note that a central feature of social supportiveness—having a pleasant personality, being easy to get along with—was almost never mentioned in connection with any of the three groups of well-known heroes. Because of the lack of sustained, close-at-hand observation and interaction, it may be difficult for young people to determine if a distant, public figure has a pleasant personality. We will see shortly that this aspect of social supportiveness was more salient for personal acquaintances.

Celebrity shallowness was used to describe athletes somewhat less often than entertainers, but considerably more often than political or military leaders. Kahn (1979) found that youths' conceptions of a wide assortment of famous heroes included substantial prominence of this quality. None of the three groups of famous heroes in the Greensboro study were characterized as strongly with celebrity shallowness as the heroes were in this earlier work. But the two groups predicted by the pessimists to possess particularly large amounts of shallowness—athletes and entertainers—were more often characterized this way in the Greensboro study. Comparatively, the characteristic was more salient for entertainers.

Negative characteristics were not used much in descriptions of any of the three groups of heroes—suggesting the existence of only small amounts of flawed complexity—but we must remember that the structure of the Greensboro study likely led respondents to underreport negative qualities. Also, several differences in characterizations noted for boys and girls, and for black and white youths, suggest compartmentalization. But results concerning flawed complexity and compartmentalization are sketchy. More work on youths' characterizations of athletic heroes related to both of these areas seems warranted.

If we return briefly to the debate about the continued existence of athletic heroes, we see that the evidence suggests a middle ground. Considering the three characteristics central in the debate, most of the evidence pertains to shallowness. Athletes are most frequently characterized in somewhat flat, unidimensional ways that emphasize outstanding athletic skills, which is undeniably a rather shallow conceptualization. Still, athletic skills fall clearly into the category of personal competence, which is a traditionally heroic characteristic. Furthermore, endurance of hardships is occasionally praised in athletes, and this somewhat broadens the conception of their personal competence. They are commended only modestly for their social supportiveness (and much of this is somewhat narrowly focused on teamwork), but nevertheless this adds something to their robustness. They are also praised in modest amounts for their celebrity shallowness, and this of course lends support to those who think they have met their demise. There are hints of flawed complexity and compartmentalization, but more definitive evidence is needed. Furthermore, knowledge of compartmentalization remains problematic with regard to helping to resolve the debate because it can be used to support either side.

Personal Acquaintances Involved in Athletics Compared With Well-Known Athletes

Personal acquaintances—relatives, neighbors, friends, teachers, coaches, playground leaders, community leaders—are usually not emphasized in studies of young peoples' conceptions of athletic heroes. This is probably because personal acquaintances are a relatively small proportion of the total group of athletes viewed as heroic. We saw previously that in the Greensboro study personal acquaintances constituted between one fourth and one third of the young people's athletic heroes.

Lack of information about youths' conceptions of personally known athletic heroes is perhaps sufficient grounds to examine them. However, there are also other reasons for attending to this topic. First, personal acquaintances have the potential to be conceptualized with more depth and breadth than distant public figures because face-to-face interaction allows acquisition of more detailed knowledge (cf. Klapp, 1962, pp. 13-14). This might support the optimistic stance in the debate; personal acquaintances might often be characterized in relatively robust, holistic terms that include a variety of traditional heroic qualities. However, this more detailed knowledge might also include serious imperfections—and people with serious imperfections being identified as heroes is evidence of flawed complexity.

Second, we saw earlier that athletically inclined females and youths chosen as heroes by the young people in the Greensboro study were likely personal acquaintances. Finally, evidence suggests that teenagers overwhelmingly identify personal acquaintances as the most influential people in their lives. McCormack (1984) found that 97% of the people viewed as influential are personal acquaintances; only 3% are public figures. Questions of influence are beyond the scope of the present volume, but these data are a strong indication that personal acquaintances are extremely important.

Young people's characterizations of heroic personal acquaintances involved in athletics are compared here with their views of famous athletic heroes. I will present two types of evidence: quantitative data using the now familiar analytical categories of personal competence, social supportiveness, celebrity shallowness, negative characteristics, and miscellaneous characteristics; and qualitative data using these same categories to address youths' reasons for declining to name athletic heroes.

Frequencies of Hero Characterizations: Quantitative Analysis

As mentioned previously, most of the youths' personally known athletic heroes were involved in sport as active players, but some local coaches, as well as a few others, were also engaged in such activities as cheerleading and weight room workouts. Most played team sports, although some were active in individual or dual sports.

Personally known athletic heroes were praised for both their social supportiveness and personal competence, with the emphasis favoring social supportiveness (see Figure 3.8). When asked specifically to discuss personally known

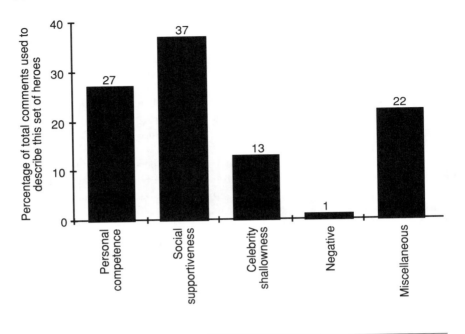

Figure 3.8.   Characterizations of personally known athletic heroes from sport-only questioning. Number of respondents = 128; frequency of comments = 82; frequency of heroes = 128.

athletic heroes, 37% of the youths' remarks concerned social supportiveness and 27% dealt with personal competence.

Social supportiveness of athletic personal acquaintances included being helpful and having a pleasant personality. Helpfulness usually concerned assistance to the young respondents themselves—taking a direct interest in nurturing them. Specifically, this included the willingness to assist them in development of their own athletic skills, to give them athletic equipment, and to take them to sports facilities. Their helpfulness often extended beyond sport to such activities as helping respondents to learn and providing them with life's necessities. Having a pleasant personality encompassed being fun to be with and not being gruff or mean to respondents. This quality also extended beyond athletics.

Personal competence mainly included exceptional athletic talent tied to ability to win games, as well as minor attention to enduring the hardships necessary to become an outstanding player. Hardships primarily concerned giving up other activities and putting in the practice time to become a good player. Showing expertise and endurance of hardships also extended beyond athletics.

Celebrity shallowness was considerably less prominent than social supportiveness and personal competence in conceptualizations of personally known athletic heroes (see Figure 3.8). Only 13% of the remarks dealt with shallowness.

Observations focused primarily on fame rather than on physical appearance or association with teams or sports valued by respondents. Local athletes derived much of their celebrity shallowness from fame within their own community or region.

Negative characterizations of personally known athletic heroes were very infrequent, comprising only 1% of the comments (see Figure 3.8). Observations involved such things as lack of athletic talent (or not developing talent fully), bad temper, and poor sportsmanship. Negative characteristics did not often extend beyond athletics.

We can make some interesting comparisons between the youths' conceptions of famous athletic heroes (see Figures 3.1 and 3.2) and personally known ones (see Figure 3.8). Personal competence was clearly the most prominent praiseworthy quality in famous athletes. By contrast, in perceptions of personal acquaintances this characteristic was less important than social supportiveness.

Also, personal competence and social supportiveness were defined somewhat differently for the two groups. Social supportiveness of well-known athletes concerned mainly teamwork and helping one's team to win. For personal acquaintances, social supportiveness was concerned primarily with the young respondents themselves: helping them become involved in sport, providing assistance to them outside of sport, and being a fun person to be with.

Celebrity shallowness was used only slightly less often in characterizing personally known athletic heroes than in characterizing famous athletes. Of course overall it was not used extensively for either group. Well-known athletes were praised for their association with favorite teams and sports, as well as for their fame, with somewhat greater emphasis placed on the former. By contrast, fame (regionally limited) was the most frequently noted aspect of celebrity shallowness for personal acquaintances involved in athletics.

Respondents mentioned few negative characteristics for either famous athletes or personally known athletes, but the comments were similar, dealing mainly with bad temper, lack of sportsmanship, questionable athletic talent, and an occasional lack of broader capabilities beyond athletics.

We should also note gender and race comparisons. First let's look at gender. I pointed out earlier that no difference was seen between the boys' and girls' conceptions of famous athletes. There was also no difference in their conceptions of personal acquaintances involved in athletics. For both of these groups of athletic heroes, the boys' and girls' perceptions followed the patterns of the full sample previously discussed. Comparing characterizations simultaneously on the basis of gender of respondents and gender of heroes would be desirable, but the boys selected very few personally known female athletic heroes, so such a comparison was not possible.

Neither was it feasible to compare the youths' conceptions of personally known black and white athletic heroes because we did not inquire about the race of these individuals (to avoid a possible source of bias; see Appendix A). However, the black youths' and white youths' overall conceptions of their personally known athletic heroes were similar and followed the patterns previously noted for the full sample.

Reasons for Declining to Name Athletic Heroes: Qualitative Analysis

We learned earlier that a substantial proportion of the Greensboro youths declined to identify athletic heroes. Twenty-four percent named no famous athletes as heroes, and 48% refused to select athletically inclined heroic personal acquaintances. By the same token, it is clear that many of the young people did name athletic heroes; only 18% identified none whatsoever. We can gain useful information about perceptions of athletic heroes by considering the reasons some respondents declined to name them. Here we compare famous athletes and personal acquaintances involved in athletics. For the most part respondents discussed negative qualities that they perceived as barriers to hero status; these mainly concerned limitations in the areas of personal competence, social supportiveness, and celebrity shallowness.

Athletes whom respondents knew personally were denied hero status most often because of personal competence limitations. In spite of strong personal competence defined by athletic talent and endurance of hardships to become good in athletics, these ''nonheroes'' lacked the extreme perseverance and the great deeds expected of heroes. Sometimes respondents conveyed in their comments that a hero must be more than just a good athlete.

> The only thing he's done good in my eyes is win the state championship, which takes a lot of practice and stuff.
> He really puts his time into track and he's really good, but he's not really what I want him to be like. I don't really look up to him.
> They haven't done anything really great.
> I look up to 'em because of their athletic ability, but I wouldn't look up to 'em as my heroes.
> I doubt they will be heroes. They will be professional athletes. There are people that I know that are good in sports . . . but these guys stole the show, they were just really excellent.
> Even though they're real good friends of mine, I guess they're just too common, ordinary people. . . . They haven't done anything out of the ordinary that nobody else has done before.
> If [she] wanted to be a real good tennis player, then she would have to work real hard. She's pretty good, but she's not the best tennis player in the world right now. Even though [my other friend] can skate good, he's not the best skater I've ever seen. They would have to work more on what they do. . . . I like them the way they are, but to be real heroes they would have to work harder in the sports that they do.
> They would have to be a little more dedicated.

The social supportiveness of personal acquaintances involved in athletics was also questionable in terms of hero status. Although these people were viewed as very good at nurturing athletic involvement of the young people in their family or community, respondents had reservations about considering them heroes because they were not involved in providing widespread, more consequential help to a larger number of people. Here are some of the comments on social supportiveness:

> *They would have to share their talents with other people.*
> *Heroes should be somebody who does something for a lot of people, and even though they've done something for me, they still haven't done something for the large majority of people.*
> *They influence a small circle of friends . . . people they know, but not a whole lot of people.*

Celebrity shallowness was also a factor in respondents declining to name heroes among athletic personal acquaintances. It was observed that personally known athletes were not famous enough to be called heroes. In addition, some respondents were not interested in sport or did not care about a particular sport. These are some of their comments:

> *So far, they're still in high school . . . and they don't get too much publicity. When they . . . get out, then they'll become stars.*
> *They are not known by many people. Maybe people like the coaches are known by people at school, but they are not known nationwide or anything.*
> *She doesn't play on TV, or something like that.*
> *Not too many people know him.*
> *If I'd look at their other qualities, they would be heroes to me, but sportwise not really, 'cause I really wouldn't want to do some of the things. Like I wouldn't want to do what [my friend] does. Her sport wouldn't interest me.*
> *They're not well-known by other people.*

Respondents' reasons for declining to call famous athletes heroes were similar to their reservations regarding athletic personal acquaintances. The most frequent observations again concerned limitations on personal competence, involving the idea that outstanding athletic performances were not important enough to be called heroic. Famous athletes were not faulted for failing to work hard, however (as several personal acquaintances were). Here are comments to show how some respondents felt about famous athletes:

> *They're just in sports. They don't do anything that's really heroic.*
> *They're just . . . athletes to me. The best athletes in their field.*
> *I don't see sports being enough to actually make somebody a hero.*
> *They only become famous in the game of sports.*
> *You can't really tell how a person is by the way he coaches basketball.*

Jimmy Black and James Worthy are close to my age. . . . They have not really gotten up in their lives . . . to be something to call them heroes.

Limitations on social supportiveness of famous athletes centered on their failure to provide broad help beyond the realm of sport. In addition, there were some observations about unpleasant personal qualities:

The only thing I really consider somebody being a hero is when they . . . save somebody's life. . . . That's really the only heroic thing, I think.
[To be a hero,] they would have to do something outside of [sport] . . . that doesn't have anything to do with money, or they'd have to do something for other people besides themselves. . . . You see these commercials every once in a while about somebody who's a sport star that's working for the United Way or crippled children or something.
They don't really help nobody, and a couple of 'em are selfish athletes.
He's a good tennis player . . . but . . . the way he acts makes me sick.

Finally, in declining to name famous athletes as heroes, some respondents' comments suggested celebrity shallowness. As might be expected, this occurred less frequently for well-known athletes than for personal acquaintances. In addition, the focus was almost exclusively on respondents' dislike of athletics and the athletes' association with this undesirable phenomenon:

I know I don't pull for Carolina, but I guess right now some of the Carolina players are [heroes]. People always talk about them, but it's not really what I'm interested in.
I don't like sports that much.

Related to this, some of the younger children—especially the 3rd graders—were almost oblivious to the world of sport. They seemed to have had little exposure to athletics and so could not think of any athletes to consider as candidates for inclusion as heroes.

Summary and Implications: Heroic Personal Acquaintances Involved in Athletics Compared With Heroic Well-Known Athletes

Earlier we saw that famous athletic heroes were not characterized by the Greensboro youths as completely shallow; descriptions included a modest amount of traditional heroism—derived primarily from personal competence. However, personal competence, for the most part, was limited to outstanding athletic talent and consequent ability to win, with secondary recognition of the hardships endured to achieve athletic greatness.

By comparison, heroic personal acquaintances involved in athletics were conceptualized with more depth and breadth. The greatest emphasis was on social supportiveness, accompanied by strong attention to personal competence. This finding is congruent with the findings of Csikszentmihalyi and Lyons (1982) showing relatively equal praise of both of these characteristics in a broad collection of personal acquaintances, and greater attention to personal competence in praiseworthy public figures.

Social supportiveness of personal acquaintances involved in athletics was defined in relatively broad terms, compared to the ways in which famous athletes were described. This characteristic encompassed helpfulness toward the young respondents themselves, as well as pleasant personality features. Both social supportiveness and personal competence are traditional heroic qualities. Notwithstanding the clear but low-level presence of celebrity shallowness in conceptions of both groups, the athletic personal acquaintances were characterized in somewhat more traditionally heroic ways than the famous athletes. We should remember, however, that a large proportion of athletic heroes are famous people rather than personal acquaintances.

In examining respondents' reasons for declining to name athletic heroes it is clear that both groups of athletes lacked some of the traditional elements of heroic greatness. They were criticized for their narrow personal competence: Great deeds of both famous and personally known ''true heroes'' were thought to extend broadly into other areas of life beyond athletics; in the case of personal acquaintances ''true heroes'' were thought to work harder to achieve their goals. Both sets of athletes were also censured for their lack of social supportiveness. Respondents thought that both famous and personally known ''true heroes'' would venture outside of athletics to offer help to people in need. Remember, however, that this negative, critical perspective was clearly a minority position. Only a small proportion of respondents chose not to name any athletic heroes at all.

Overall, the youths' conceptions appear to support a middle-of-the-road stance regarding the debate over the continued existence of athletic heroes. For most of the Greensboro youths athletic heroes continued to exist. They were readily identified by many, and they were defined in ways that were neither completely shallow nor completely robust with regard to traditional heroic greatness. Heroes were thought to possess a small amount of flawed complexity as evidenced by occasional references to negative characteristics such as unpleasant personalities, poor sportsmanship, or less than spectacular athletic talents. In addition, a few differences between the black and white youths regarding their characterizations of famous athletes hint at a small amount of compartmentalized appeal. Knowledge of the latter remains less helpful for progressing toward resolving the debate, however, because such data can be used to support either the pessimists' or the optimists' position.

Now that we are familiar with youths' athletic hero choices and characterizations, we can combine these two sets of information to address the debate as comprehensively as possible.

Chapter 4

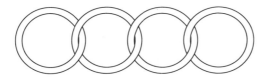

Toward Resolution of the Dilemma

The dilemma concerning the ongoing existence of heroes in American society has been evident since at least the 1950s and has remained prominent through the 1980s. In the midst of this controversy, highly talented athletes have come under sharp criticism. Along with entertainers, athletes are identified by the pessimists as prime examples of deteriorating heroes. The optimists disagree. Their position is that although many characteristics of contemporary athletic heroes differ from those of their historical counterparts, today's heroes nevertheless remain robust, viable figures with traditionally heroic qualities.

The debate has continued over the last several decades. Perhaps it is destined to extend into the foreseeable future, taking various twists and turns as events occur to make one of the two positions more tenable, or to give more salience to the overall debate. Ongoing social change may prevent the debate from ever being completely settled.

Progress toward a definitive answer has been hampered by lack of evidence concerning conceptions of athletic heroes held by the American public. Analysts have generally been content to carry out social and historical appraisals that support their initial optimistic or pessimistic assumptions. They have not been particularly concerned about corroborating their claims against what the general public might think, which is important because the general public is involved in defining and selecting heroes—both public figures and personal acquaintances. Of course the mass media and many other social institutions are also influential, but widespread, active involvement by individuals is a significant factor. When the focus is on athletic heroes, the opinions of young people are especially relevant because they select more athletes as heroes than adults do.

The major goal of the current volume has been to examine research concerning youths' athletic hero choices and their characterizations of the athletic heroes they select. In previous chapters I have presented and discussed the available evidence regarding athletic heroes and the ways they are characterized by youths.

My aim now is to apply this evidence toward resolving the debate. I will also point out ways in which the debate remains unsettled and suggest further research that would aid our understanding.

Contributions Toward Resolving the Debate

A summary of the types of evidence that support the optimistic and pessimistic extremes appears in Tables 4.1 and 4.2. Information about athletic hero *choices* at first seems to provide direct evidence of the extent to which heroes exist. By itself, however, knowledge of hero choices does not help us very much in moving toward resolving the debate because it can be interpreted to support either side.

An indication of the extent to which heroes exist can be obtained by counting the number of heroes identified, and by comparing the proportion of people who name heroes with those who decline to designate them. Of course methodological safeguards to legitimate either answer are necessary. If many heroes are named, or if a high proportion of people acknowledge having heroes, such results would fuel the optimists. Beyond mere numbers, the collective breadth of heroes identified might ensure some level of traditional heroism. The pessimists would counter,

Table 4.1 Hero Choices: Types of Evidence Used to Support Optimistic and Pessimistic Extremes

	Optimistic position	Pessimistic position
Number of heroes identified	Many	Many
		Few
Proportion of people who identify heroes	High	High
		Low
Shallowness	Long-lived[a]	Long-lived[a]
	Short-lived	Short-lived
Flawed complexity	Short-lived	Short-lived
Compartmentalization	High variation	High variation
	Short-lived	Short-lived

Note. In cases where contradictory evidence supports the same position, or where the same evidence supports both positions, different interpretations are used to make the evidence congruent with the position(s). Such evidence is less helpful for resolving the debate because it can be interpreted in more than one way.

[a]There is little evidence of long-lived public acclaim for contemporary heroes.

Table 4.2   Hero Characterizations: Types of Evidence Used to Support Optimistic and Pessimistic Extremes

	Optimistic position	Pessimistic position
Shallowness	Low-frequency celebrity shallowness High-frequency negative celebrity shallowness[a] High-frequency personal competence High-frequency social supportiveness	High-frequency celebrity shallowness Low-frequency negative celebrity shallowness[a] Low-frequency personal competence Low-frequency social supportiveness
Flawed complexity[b]	Low-frequency negative personal competence[a] Low-frequency negative social supportiveness[a] Low-frequency other negative qualities[a]	High-frequency negative personal competence[a] High-frequency negative social supportiveness[a] High-frequency other negative qualities[a]
Compartmentalization	High variation	High variation

Note. In cases where contradictory evidence supports the same position, or where the same evidence supports both positions, different interpretations are used to make the evidence congruent with the position(s). Such evidence is less helpful for resolving the debate because it can be interpreted in more than one way.

[a]There is little evidence of negative characterizations of contemporary heroes; [b]Flawed complexity is useful for resolving the debate only when negative characterizations are evaluated as negative by respondents.

however, that the shallow, flawed, compartmentalized characteristics of these individuals make them unworthy of heroic status. Thus, information about naming or declining to name heroes provides little solid evidence to help settle the debate.

If particular heroes appeal to specific groups, it follows that there would also be differences in these groups' hero selection patterns—which would indicate compartmentalization. Short-lived appeal is also relevant here because rapid turnover may facilitate the development of compartmentalization. As we know, however, compartmentalized appeal can support either the optimists or the pessimists. Short-lived appeal is also considered to indicate flawed complexity by the pessimists, but the optimists view this trait as a mark of vitality. Short-lived appeal is also thought by the pessimists to mark heroic shallowness. The optimists of course remain steadfast in viewing this trait as indicating diversity and liveliness. Interestingly, long-lived appeal can also be used to support either side on the question of shallowness. The key is whether long-lived heroes are viewed as traditional heroes or hollow celebrities.

Knowledge of athletic hero *characterizations* is directly applicable to considerations of all three problematic characteristics. Some of this evidence can be valuable in helping to resolve the debate. It can also be used to give greater relevance to the hero choice data.

Most of the available information concerns shallowness. If heroes are seen as vibrant and robust with traditional heroic qualities, we would have difficulty justifying charges of shallowness. On the other hand, if they are conceptualized as limited and narrow with little beyond flashy and glittering surface qualities, then claims of shallowness might be supportable. A person being viewed as heroic despite negative perceptions by respondents about celebrity shallowness (e.g., not good-looking or not very famous) also suggests a more traditional conception.

It is important to avoid relying on independent judgments from external analysts about what constitutes a flaw. When external opinions are employed, the result is information that can be used to the advantage of either side. Characteristics the pessimists consider flaws are often not seen that way by the optimists. Our goal is to determine the extent to which the general public views particular qualities of their heroes as negative. However, such information is limited and fragmentary. What little there is comes mainly from the Greensboro study.

Differences among specific groups concerning the ways they characterize heroes, including whether or not their heroes have negative characteristics, might indicate compartmentalization. But as we know, information about compartmentalized appeal does not help us move toward a solution to the debate because it can be used to the advantage of either side. Furthermore, our knowledge of such disagreements is fragmentary, coming mostly from the Greensboro study.

Considering the types of information just discussed, the best evidence currently available for helping to resolve the debate concerns shallowness and its counterpoint, traditional heroism. In the context of these aspects of hero characterizations, information about hero choices takes on additional meaning. If most heroes are characterized in shallow ways, this would support the pessimists, whereas traditional characterizations would support the optimists.

Let's briefly recap what we know about shallowness and traditional heroism of athletes. For simplicity I will refer collectively to athletes judged heroic and/ or admirable as "heroes." An overall look is followed by specific discussions of gender, race, and grade in school.

Shallowness and Traditional Heroism

Famous athletic heroes are praised most highly for their personal competence. This trait mainly involves extraordinary athletic talent coupled with ability to win; to a lesser extent it also has to do with endurance of hardships encountered in becoming an outstanding athlete and continuing to compete at elite levels. Social supportiveness is also found in conceptions of famous athletic heroes, but only in modest amounts and focusing mainly on helping one's team to win. Finally, modest attention is given to celebrity shallowness in association with valued teams and sports, along with widespread fame.

By contrast, personally known athletic heroes are commended more equally for personal competence and social supportiveness, with somewhat greater emphasis on the latter. In addition, both of these qualities are perceived to extend beyond athletics. Similar to famous athletes, for personally known athletic heroes personal competence is defined with primary emphasis on athletic talent and less emphasis on endurance of hardships. However, the conception of social supportiveness differs. For personal acquaintances, it centers on nurturing activities that help respondents get involved in sport. It also involves a variety of pleasant personality features that make people fun to be with. Finally, there is a modest focus on celebrity shallowness, as with well-known athletes; for personal acquaintances celebrity shallowness involves fame almost exclusively.

From this standpoint, young people conceive athletic heroes as being neither completely shallow (as the pessimists suggest) nor completely traditional (as the optimists suggest). If we look at both personal competence and social supportiveness, we see that personally known athletes are characterized in broader, more traditionally heroic ways than famous athletes. But when we look only at personal competence of famous athletes, we see that even they are not completely empty of traditional heroism.

Let's now situate the information about hero characterizations in the context of what we know about hero choices. Personal acquaintances account for a relatively small proportion of athletic heroes; the rest are public figures. Because most athletic heroes are famous, most would be attributed the narrow, less traditionally heroic features just summarized. However, we need to remember that personal acquaintances are reportedly more influential on young people's lives than popular, famous figures. Perhaps the smaller number of personally known athletic heroes is disproportionately influential.

We should also remember that famous athletes constitute a visible but limited proportion of the total set of young people's famous heroes. The others—primarily entertainers and political or military leaders—are characterized more frequently than athletes as socially supportive, and their social support often involves broad help to society or to specific groups who face major problems. Personal competence is also salient in conceptualizations of both these other types of heroes. But celebrity shallowness is considerable for entertainers, and this offsets some of their traditional heroism. Celebrity shallowness is almost completely absent in conceptions of political or military leaders.

Famous athletes seem to be defined with salient amounts of shallowness, especially in comparison with political or military leaders. They seem less traditionally heroic and yet are not completely lacking in traditional heroism. Political or military leaders have the most traditionally heroic profile: exceptionally strong social supportiveness, quite strong personal competence, and almost no celebrity shallowness. Because they constitute a rather small proportion of famous heroes, however, their impact may be considerably diluted by much larger numbers of entertainers and athletes with somewhat more questionable characterizations in terms of traditional heroism.

Gender, Race, and Grade in School

Clearly, American society is made up of many different groups with widely different life experiences, perceptions, and opinions. If we compare these it might shed light on diversities and similarities that exist regarding hero characterizations and hero choices. Here we continue our focus on shallowness and traditional heroism, making comparisons based on gender, race, and grade in school. Knowledge is somewhat fragmentary, so examination of the same topics in each type of comparison is not possible. In some cases I will offer my speculations as logical extensions of the existing evidence.

It is important to recognize that comparisons at the level of gender, race, and grade are quite coarse-grained. It would be helpful if additional data become available in the future permitting examination of such subgroups as rural black females in the Southeast, Hispanics in the Southwest, gay men, Puerto Rican immigrants in New York City, working-class women, intact friendship groups or subcultures, black male teenagers in Los Angeles, Korean immigrants on the West Coast, or admirers of some particular hero or type of hero.

We turn first to gender comparisons. Girls' athletic hero choices include more personal acquaintances then those of boys, whereas boys name more famous public figures. Both genders name more public figures overall. Girls' and boys' conceptions of famous and personally known athletes are similar. Since girls' athletic hero choices include a greater proportion of personal acquaintances, however, it seems reasonable to speculate that girls' conceptions of their total set of athletic heroes may be more congruent with the ways in which they characterize their personally known athletic heroes. We know that personally known athletic heroes are defined in more traditionally heroic ways than famous athletic heroes. Overall, then, girls may hold a somewhat more traditionally heroic view of athletic heroes than boys.

Race comparisons are limited to examination of blacks and whites. The most interesting comparison concerns the total group of famous heroes, rather than famous athletes in particular. Black and white youths both tend to identify relatively equal numbers of athletes, entertainers, and political or military leaders among famous heroes of their own race, although the tendency is stronger for blacks. The tendency is also for both black and white youths to emphasize personal competence and social supportiveness rather equally in characterizations of famous same-race heroes. Perhaps the fairly even mixture of the three types of famous same-race heroes partially explains the relatively even mixture of the two characterizations.

Choices and characterizations of famous opposite-race heroes cannot be interrelated quite so neatly. White youths include a preponderance of athletes among their black heroes, and black youths include a preponderance of entertainers among their white heroes, but the tendency is stronger for whites. Famous athletes tend to be characterized with more emphasis on personal competence, which might be why white youths' characterizations of famous opposite-race heroes focus more heavily on this quality. Famous entertainers tend to be characterized with closer to equal amounts of personal competence and social supportiveness, which perhaps contributes to black youths' greater emphasis on social supportiveness in opposite-race heroes.

The more broad-based distributions of choices and characterizations among same-race heroes, along with the more skewed distributions of both of these among opposite-race heroes, suggests that same-race heroes may be conceptualized in broader and thus more traditionally heroic ways. Opposite-race heroes certainly do not completely lack traditionally heroic qualities: Black youths heavily praise white heroes for their social supportiveness, and white youths strongly commend black heroes for their personal competence. However, opposite-race heroes seem to be characterized with somewhat less breadth—particularly black heroes identified by white youths. Almost all black heroes picked by whites are athletes, with an exceptionally heavy focus on their personal competence centered on athletic talent (heavier than the generally strong focus on this quality for athletes overall).

There is one broader age comparison extending beyond school-aged youths that we should note, along with several comparisons among 3rd, 6th, 9th, and 12th graders. Children and adolescents tend to select more athletes and entertainers as heroes, whereas adults choose more political or military leaders. Youths' characterizations of athletic heroes fall somewhere between the extremes of total shallowness and totally traditional heroism. Based on adults' frequent choices of political or military leaders, and assuming their characterizations of these individuals resemble those of young people, we can speculate that adults' hero characterizations would be oriented strongly toward social supportiveness and personal competence. In other words, they would tend to emphasize traditional heroism more than young people do.

Among heroic athletes selected by children and adolescents, 6th and 9th graders select larger proportions of famous athletes and smaller proportions of personally known ones. By comparison, the proportion of well-known athletes is smaller for 3rd and 12th graders. These data can be placed in the context of the different characterizations of famous and personally known athletic heroes. Famous athletes are conceptualized with greater shallowness and less traditional heroism than athletic personal acquaintances. Because middle-graders tend to select more famous athletes, we can speculate that their views of athletic heroes may be somewhat less traditionally heroic.

We move now to consider youths' choices of famous heroes from all walks of life. Younger children—3rd graders—choose a heavy preponderance of entertainers among their famous heroes. Middle-graders—6th and 9th—select a mixture of athletes, entertainers, and political or military leaders, with a substantially heavier focus on athletes and entertainers. Older adolescents—12th graders—distribute their heroes about equally between (a) athletes and entertainers, and (b) political or military leaders and others such as scientists, humanitarians, and explorers. We should not be surprised to see that choices of 12th graders resemble adults' choices more than choices of younger students do.

Based on knowledge of the ways the three main groups of heroes are characterized, we might suppose that because of the greater variety of heroes chosen by 6th, 9th, and 12th graders, they would all be likely to conceive of their total set of heroes in more traditionally heroic ways than 3rd graders. Entertainers, of course, tend to be conceptualized with a moderate amount of traditional heroism, so even 3rd graders' conceptions—based on their heavy focus on entertainers—would include a degree of this traditionalism. But entertainers also are perceived to have a moderate amount of celebrity shallowness, and this would undoubtedly be salient in 3rd graders' perceptions. Furthermore, due to 12th graders' somewhat less frequent choice of athletes and entertainers— the two groups of heroes characterized with the most celebrity shallowness—they might conceive of their heroes more traditionally.

Resolution of the Debate Remains Elusive

It is clear that in the 1980s young people still identified athletes as heroes and characterized them somewhere between the extremes of shallowness and traditional heroism. To the extent that personal acquaintances were included among athletic heroes, conceptions were probably more traditionally heroic. But many youths declined to name athletic heroes who were personal acquaintances. Characterizations of at least one set of heroes—political or military leaders—were more robust and traditionally heroic than those of athletes. Entertainers were also defined with a broader range of traditional heroism, but their characterizations included substantial shallowness, which may have negated some of their greater robustness. All told, conceptions of athletes and entertainers both seem to have been located midway between the two extremes. A handful of gender, race, and grade comparisons suggest some differences, but more work is needed to confirm and extend this knowledge.

This evidence is somewhat equivocal in terms of helping resolve the scholarly and journalistic debate about the continued existence of athletic heroes. Youths' choices of heroes and characterizations of them do not offer definitive support for one side or the other. In fact, their middle-of-the-road position may serve to fuel the debate rather than settle it. The pessimists might charge that my findings are evidence of ambivalence and uncertainty about the nature of athletic heroes—definitely not the sort of characterizations one would expect in connection with strong, traditionally heroic figures. But the optimists might argue that the findings confirm a moderate amount of traditionally heroic vibrancy because athletic heroes are not perceived to be completely shallow.

Our knowledge of American youths' midway position can also be used to speculate about their broader opinions of society. Recall that the debate about heroes is rooted in a larger issue—whether American society is disillusioned and deteriorating or viable and diverse. Youths' moderate position on heroes suggests that they might hold a similarly middle-ground assumption about American society—that it is neither in danger of extensive decline nor about to experience a vibrant renaissance.

Perhaps it is important to remember that the middle position of young people is an amalgam of all their choices and characterizations. The same sort of position would probably appear if we were to mix together all the views of the pessimists and optimists. We can speculate that there are strong optimists and pessimists among children and adolescents in American society just as there are among journalists and scholars. Maybe the analysts and the youths reflect each other. It is clear that mutual influences occur between the mass media and those who watch, listen, and read (cf. Condit, 1989; Fiske, 1987). Many journalists and broadcasters undoubtedly influence youths' conceptions of athletic heroes, and in turn the special twists that young people give to heroes through their interpretations sometimes filter back to influence the media.

Note that the *continued* existence of athletic heroes is at the crux of the debate. Unfortunately no evidence has been found concerning youths' characterizations of athletic heroes before the late 1950s or early 1960s, the purported period of their demise. Nor is there much information from the later 1960s and 1970s about youths' characterizations. Broad-based findings are available from earlier periods of the 20th century concerning choices of heroes and other admirable people (Averill, 1950; Greenstein, 1969), and we also know that evidence about choices in the 1970s and 1980s is fairly plentiful. Without knowledge of characterizations, however, it is impossible to determine whether youths' conceptions in the 1980s were markedly different from what young people thought in earlier years.

The debate will likely persist in the future, heating up, cooling down, and ramifying in various ways as national and international events unfold. Additional research concerning youths' athletic hero choices and characterizations might add clarity to the situation; in the following I will suggest what kind of investigations are needed.

Further Resolution of the Debate

We have seen that youths' athletic hero choices, taken by themselves, are of little use in addressing the debate. Athletic hero characterizations are much more helpful. So in terms of progressing further, future research should focus on collecting more detailed and comprehensive information about young people's conceptions of athletic heroes, coupled with a record of the people they choose. We should continue to look both at famous athletes and at athletic personal acquaintances. These should also be compared with their counterparts—both famous and personally known—from other walks of life. Athletes from different sports should also be compared. Before recommending specific research that would help address the debate, I want to make three relatively general observations.

First, heroes are assumed to have various kinds of influence on individuals and society. They are thought to be important in several ways: in helping people develop definitions of individual and collective identity; in displaying ideal ways of behaving that can be emulated; in compensating for deficiencies in individuals and in the broader society; and in providing temporary escape from the problems of everyday life. However, little research exists to document these influences.

Caughey's (1984) examination of imaginary social relationships that people develop with distant media figures and personal acquaintances is relevant here and can be set in the context of several levels of heroic influence posited by McEvoy and Erickson (1981). These are defined in terms of the intensity of five admirer actions: (1) admiration of heroes; (2) identification with heroes; (3) utilization of heroes as "standards for self-appraisals and appraisals of others"; (4) imitation of heroes' actions; and (5) acting as an advocate on behalf of heroes (pp. 117-119).

Caughey (1984) points to fan clubs as evidence of specific influence of media figures on behavior of admirers (p. 63). Within the framework of McEvoy and Erickson (1981), involvement in fan club activities falls within the fifth influence level: acting as an advocate of a hero, sacrificing one's own time and energy to further the hero and whatever she or he represents.

The first two levels suggested by McEvoy and Erickson (1981), admiration and the emotional attachment and empathy that characterize identification, are also amply supported by evidence from Caughey (1984).

> People express strong emotional orientations to . . . [media] figures, speaking not only of "admiration" and "sympathy," but also of "worship" and (platonic) "love" . . . people frequently characterize the attraction by comparing it to a real social relationship. They speak of their hero as a "friend," "older sister," "father figure," "guide" or "mentor" . . . the emotional attachment is not complicated by the ambivalence that characterizes actual relationships; admiration is unchecked by the recognition of faults and limitations. (p. 53)

Use of a media figure as an ideal for appraising one's self and others, the third level in the McEvoy and Erickson (1981) model, is also demonstrated in one of Caughey's (1984) examples, particularly relevant to appraisal of others.

> One man pointed out that the "father figure" he admired—a fictional John Wayne-type TV cowboy—outshone his real father in every respect. His father has several admirable qualities and he "loves him very much." But as a child he "needed someone to identify with," and his father did not measure up. (pp. 53-54)

Using a media figure as a standard to appraise one's own self appears to be closely linked with imitation, the fourth level in the McEvoy and Erickson framework. It seems a short leap from comparative self-appraisal to actual imitative behavior. Caughey suggests that three types of imaginary relationships involve admiration of media figures, the final two clearly involving imitation: meeting the person and establishing "a close and intimate social relationship"

(p. 56); taking on characteristics similar to the media figure, becoming someone who "lives out experiences similar to those of the idol" (p. 57); and actually becoming the media figure to the point that "in fantasy, the individual's consciousness is 'possessed' by the media self; it colors perception, patterns decision making, and structures social behavior" (p. 58). A hero's appearance and values may also influence a fan's actual appearance and behavior, as well as his or her fantasies.

Caughey (1984) also suggests that media figures influence fans' actual lives in ways that do not fall neatly within the McEvoy and Erickson (1981) model. For example, norms are developed that govern interaction when live people and media figures are present in a room simultaneously, members of fan clubs have a ready-made basis for social interaction among themselves, and fans may experience sneers and derision from others who learn about the pervasiveness of their fantasy attachments.

Caughey's (1984) study extends beyond media figures, documenting the extent to which our ongoing lives are permeated by imaginary relationships with a host of others—live public figures and personal acquaintances, as well as newly created, wholly fantasized characters. This extensive penetration of imaginary relationships into ongoing social life in itself can be considered an important effect of intense involvement with heroes. Although Caughey believes that most imaginary relationships are a normal, healthy part of life, there may also be negative consequences, including imitation of behaviors usually considered antisocial, such as "violence, selfishness, predatory sexuality, and materialism" (p. 248), as well as occasional pathological, psychiatric effects.

Though our knowledge about influences of heroes is somewhat limited, additional help is available from broader areas of scholarship dealing with socializing influences of the people most commonly perceived as heroes and the social settings in which they are found. The following two areas of study would be particularly useful: influences of personal acquaintances and associated institutions—families, peers, and educational settings; and influences of mass cultural performances—television, film, popular music, athletics, and political activities.

McCormack (1984) points out that a high percentage of the individuals identified by teenagers as influential in their lives are personal acquaintances. Yet a large proportion of young people's heroes are well known. Perhaps influences of public figures are relatively tacit and less consciously acknowledged by admirers than influences of face-to-face acquaintances. Whatever the case, additional work on influences of athletic heroes seems warranted.

A second preliminary observation is that little is known about the process by which heroes come into being. We know that the process involves complex relationships among the candidates for hero status, the mass media (in the case of public figures), and the people who come to admire them (Rein et al., 1987). Gamson (1992) points to a shift during the 20th century from media accounts emphasizing the importance of talent and virtue in rising to the top to more recent media reports exposing the publicity apparatus that can transform anyone into a famous celebrity. It is an active, dynamic process. As with all of social life, power differences among individuals and groups are important. Some of the key factors in the process are examined in Goode's (1978) study of prestige as a system of social control. Loy and Hesketh (1984) suggest that heroic greatness among athletes is still partially rooted in remnants of an agonal system dating back to ancient Greece. Clearly, more specific research on the development of athletic heroes would be helpful.

Heroic action is dynamic. It involves performing great deeds; enduring hardships; helping others; maintaining a friendly, easygoing personality; and mixing in an occasional sprinkle of glittering performances where exquisite outer images are on display. Yet youths' characterizations of athletic heroes have been studied as if people were static. Respondents have been asked to describe heroes at a single point in time without concern for the ongoing flow of life activities. A third recommendation, then, is that future research should include questioning designed to encourage more dynamic characterizations. Topics might include activities of a particular hero throughout a recent period of time, perhaps a year or two; activities of a particular hero throughout a short string of related events such as the World Series or the Wimbledon tennis tournament; real or imaginary interactions between admirers and their heroes; or the life history of a particular hero. Respondents could be asked to recount such events in as much detail as possible.

A number of specific suggestions can be made concerning additional information about young people and their athletic heroes that might clarify various dimensions of the debate. Recalling the three counts by which the pessimists condemn athletic heroes—shallowness, flawed complexity, and compartmentalization—we have seen that examining shallowness has been of greatest service. In the Greensboro study it was useful to set celebrity shallowness against two groups of traditionally heroic characteristics—personal competence and social supportiveness. Yet our knowledge of the amount of shallowness and traditional heroism in youths' conceptions of praiseworthy athletes remains limited. Additional work is needed to confirm the results of the Greensboro study, point out changes that may occur in future years, and provide more fine-grained knowledge of young people's conceptions of personal competence, social supportiveness, celebrity shallowness, and negative characteristics.

Each of the three main characteristics in the Greensboro study is comprised of a variety of qualities that can and should be examined more closely. Personal competence involves extraordinary expertise as well as endurance of hardships. Social supportiveness concerns helpfulness, as well as possession of a pleasant, easygoing personality. Celebrity shallowness includes fame, good looks, and association with valued phenomena; wealth, although not salient in the Greensboro study, belongs in this category. Future investigations might bring additional qualities to light.

Because we are interested specifically in athletic heroes, it might be particularly fruitful to examine conceptions of extraordinary athletic talent in more detail. Separate focuses on winning and playing well were not evident in the Greensboro study, but the enormous attention given to winning in American society makes this worth another look. There might also be other qualitative differences concerning athletic talent. For example, the Greensboro study faintly suggested that boys discuss athletes' playing skills in more explicit, technical detail than girls do. It would be valuable to understand better the extent of technical sophistication in admirers' perceptions of athletic talent, as this might shed light on the degree to which playing skills and strategic capabilities are perceived as shallow, surface qualities or complex personal competencies. Such perception might also be indicative of the extent to which admirers focus rather single-mindedly on athletic talent, perhaps ignoring other facets of players' lives.

Although aggressiveness and violence are not prominent in youths' characterizations of athletic heroes, evidence shows that some people enjoy violence in sport, which suggests the likelihood that they find such qualities praiseworthy in athletes. Studies should examine this possible connection.

Aggressiveness and violence, as well as technically sophisticated details of playing skills, are qualities that might be linked theoretically to the notion of a pervasive technological ethos in American society. In both cases a disregard for athletes' holistic humanness may be present; if so, this may be tied to general societal metaphors in which humans are considered analogous to inanimate, utilitarian machines (Hoberman, 1992). Other aspects of youths' characterizations of athletic talent may also be uncovered in future work.

We have also seen that information about youths' conceptions of flawed complexity would be helpful for addressing the debate. If admirers' characterizations of athletic heroes include qualities that they themselves judge to be flaws, the pessimistic claim that heroes are no longer defined as paragons of unblemished perfection is supported. Hints of flawed complexity in the Greensboro study were manifest in occasional negative characterizations. However, there were methodological limitations that likely discouraged respondents from making negative remarks (see Appendix A and Appendix B). More information is needed about the proportion of negative comments used to characterize athletic heroes, along with details of the content. It would also help to learn about respondents' rationale for viewing people as heroic despite acknowledged flaws.

We have observed that evidence of compartmentalization is not of much help in resolving the debate because such evidence can support either side. However, we should continue to assess compartmentalization because *absence* of this characteristic in even a few athletic heroes would undermine the pessimistic stance. Former basketball star Michael Jordan's current record of 6 consecutive years among the top heroes of a national sample of American secondary school students makes him the only contemporary contender—athlete or otherwise—for broad, long-lived heroic appeal.

If various groups of respondents differ in terms of hero choices and/or characterizations (placing different emphases on celebrity shallowness, personal competence, social supportiveness, and negative characteristics), this would suggest compartmentalized appeal. In spite of the drawback inherent in the compartmentalization evidence regarding settling the debate, it remains important to gain additional insights about variations among specific groups in American society in terms of their athletic hero choices and characterizations. Our society is diverse and multifaceted—some would say splintered and sharply segmented. Relatively coarse-grained, monolithic investigations are not likely to uncover the rich variety that probably exists among members of different social formations based on factors such as race, ethnicity, gender, sexual preference, age, social class, region, and rural/urban differences. Subgroups within these larger formations (e.g., Cuban boys in Miami, girls attending elite private schools in the Northeast, rural youths in Kansas) should also be considered.

The Greensboro study demonstrated a hint of racial stereotyping in white youths' heavy selection of athletes among their black heroes. Although there was no evidence of stereotyping in black and white youths' characterizations of athletes or other heroes, there was a suggestion of greater variety in both their choices and characterizations of the broad collection of same-race heroes coming from all walks of life. Various sorts of stereotypic conceptions should be given further scholarly attention.

In spite of evidence pointing to a modest amount of compartmentalization based on gender, race, and grade differences, there is considerable similarity among young people's athletic hero choices and characterizations. This is important to remember, even if more fine-grained work uncovers additional differences in the future. Despite diverse structural locations in society, young people are not entirely different along these lines. We sometimes get so intent on looking for contrasts that we forget to acknowledge important likenesses.

This is not meant to suggest that such commonalities should be evaluated entirely positively as indicators of some sort of structural-functional "common bond" among American youths (cf. Coakley, 1990; Eitzen & Sage, 1991). From a social-conflict or cultural-studies perspective (cf. Coakley, 1990; Donnelly, Hargreaves, & Tomlinson, 1992; Eitzen & Sage, 1991) one could argue that these similarities indicate the continuing dominance of powerful groups and the pervasiveness of support for the status quo—a pervasiveness that extends even to members of subordinate groups who have less power and fewer opportunities to reshape current social arrangements more to their advantage. Future scholarly analyses of athletic heroes guided by this latter framework would be extremely fruitful.

More generally, it would be interesting to compare young people's characterizations of athletic heroes with the ways that they are portrayed by the mass media. Such work could focus on some of the factors already mentioned. It is clear that a variety of nationalistic, capitalistic, patriarchal, and racist messages were present in media coverage of sport in the 1980s (Kinkema & Harris, 1992). It might be useful to examine a hero with wide appeal such as Michael Jordan and a controversial figure with more limited appeal such as Martina Navratilova. We know that media accounts do not have simple, direct influences on audiences. Rather, within complex interaction processes media content is modified by members of the general public as they interpret it in terms of their own social circumstances and individual life histories. The media content and the people who encounter it are mutually influential (cf. Condit, 1989; Fiske, 1987), which suggests a need to compare the two.

Expanding our scope even further, it would be useful to keep track of the debate, looking at the circumstances in which it heats up, cools down, or changes course. It is possible that when external threats to American society are perceived as eminent—such as during the 1990-1991 Gulf War—the pessimists are less likely to offer their critical views about internal problems and the demise of heroes. When external perils are perceived as less acute there may be more latitude to examine internal problems such as racial tensions, national economic problems, environmental concerns, and abortion rights. In situations where external threats are less immediate perhaps the pessimists are encouraged to be more vocal. Care must be exercised in accepting this possibility, however, because some of the most strident criticisms of heroes occurred in the 1960s and 1970s during the Vietnam War.

We have experienced within recent years the political and economic reconfiguration of Eastern Europe, the Gulf War, a widespread loss of confidence in elected politicians, greater recognition of environmental problems, the continuing spread of drug use and related crime, the growth of the AIDS epidemic, growing concerns about the adequacy of our health care system, the development of rap music, challenges to the legality of abortions, an economic recession, and a growth in interethnic tensions perhaps most clearly manifested in a major riot in 1992 in south central Los Angeles. Recently, United States Vice President Dan Quayle criticized the popular television character Murphy Brown for bearing a child without plans to involve the father in its upbringing; two major sports figures—Magic Johnson and Arthur Ashe—acknowledged contracting the HIV virus; Bill Clinton played the saxophone on Arsenio Hall's late-night television show and later jammed with several bands at inaugural balls; tennis star Monica Seles was stabbed in the back by a spectator during a tournament; New York Mets baseball player Vince Coleman injured several fans when he threw lighted firecrackers at them; Phoenix Suns basketball player Charles Barkley announced in a television ad that he is not a role model; and the enormously popular Michael Jordan announced his retirement from the Chicago Bulls.

Entwined with all of this and with events that will unfold in the future, the debate about the ongoing existence of athletic heroes seems likely to continue, probably taking unpredictable directions. The prominence of the debate may wax and wane, and the central arguments may shift. For the time being, however, our knowledge of youths' hero choices and characterizations points to a middle-of-the-road position—somewhere midway between the pessimistic claim of heroic demise and the optimistic assertion of continued viability.

Appendix A

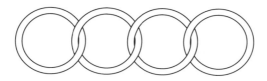

Greensboro Study: Research Methods and Design

The Greensboro study was conducted in Greensboro, North Carolina, between January and April of 1982. The details of the research methods and design are outlined in what follows; additional procedural information is included where relevant in the text.

The children and adolescents taking part were students in the Greensboro Public Schools. With the help of school officials, three institutions were selected: one elementary school, one junior high school, and one high school. The schools were similar in that each contained an adequate number of black and white students to serve as respondents, each was thought by school officials to have a similar mix of students from varying socioeconomic backgrounds, and the principals were willing to permit on-site conduct of the study.

Respondents were selected from each of four grade levels. At each grade level the sample contained an equal number of males and females, and an equal number of black and white youths. Financial and time constraints made it necessary to limit the study to 32 respondents at each grade level: eight black boys, eight black girls, eight white boys, and eight white girls. The grade levels were 3rd, 6th, 9th, and 12th. The total number of respondents was 128.

One 3rd grade class and one 6th grade class were randomly chosen from all classes at these grade levels in the participating elementary school. Students from the two classes were randomly chosen within the previously described guidelines to take part in the study. There were not enough black students in the first class selected at either grade level to fill the quota, so a second class at each grade level was randomly selected from which to draw additional respondents. Similar procedures were carried out in the other two schools. Junior high school 9th grade social studies classes were used because all 9th graders were enrolled in one of these. For the same reason high school homeroom classes were used to select the 12th graders. Informed consent to take part in the study was obtained from both the students and their parents.

If parents' education level can be accepted as an index of socioeconomic status, then the socioeconomic backgrounds of the youngsters in this investigation were related somewhat to their race. The most common indicators of socio-economic status are education, income, and occupational prestige. These three combined would provide a finer grained index than any one alone, but it was not possible to gather data concerning income and occupation of the youths' parents. Based on chi-square analyses of parents' education, the white students tended to come from more favored backgrounds. Fathers (X^2 [2, $N = 99$] = 22.91, $p \leq .001$) and mothers (X^2 [2, $N = 109$] = 17.79, $p \leq .001$) of the white students both had significantly higher levels of education than those of the black students. Among parents of white students, 43% of the fathers and 31% of the mothers had 4-year college degrees. Only 5% of the black students' fathers and 6% of their mothers had graduated from college. There were similar, but less striking, differences for high school graduation. These data suggest that racial comparisons in this investigation must be tempered with a cautionary note that they may partially reflect socioeconomic differences.

The youngsters were interviewed individually. The length of an interview varied from about 20 to 90 minutes depending on the extensiveness of a respondent's answers. Each person was asked questions about the nature and importance of people he or she considered admirable and/or heroic (see Appendix B). The interviews were semistructured and open-ended. A major goal of the study was to ascertain the youths' own conceptions of the people they considered praiseworthy, and therefore most questions permitted wide-ranging answers. The same questions were asked of each respondent, but at times there were slight variations in wording and order depending on a particular respondent's answers to preceding questions. All interviews were tape-recorded and transcribed.

The interviews were conducted during the school day. Two graduate students were trained as interviewers. They were both white females, which may have introduced an unknown amount of bias into the research. Only one fourth of the youths (the white females) had an interviewer who was of their own race and gender.

Respondents were not asked about race, gender, or age of any of the people they named (public figures or personal acquaintances) because we thought such questions might bias responses. For gender and age, independent determinations were made for both personal acquaintances and public figures. Race of public figures was also determined independently, but this was not possible for personal acquaintances. In cases where respondents named two or more people together from different categories (e.g., parents, a whole athletic team, a mixed musical group) they were placed in a category labeled "other." Also in this category were heroes for whom gender, race, or age could not be determined and members of racial groups other than black or white.

Each interview was divided into two main parts: Initially we asked a respondent to discuss praiseworthy people in general; then we discussed sport specifically (see Table A.1). The sport-specific questions often elicited additional names of athletes unmentioned in the general section of the interview. However, in other cases respondents did not rename athletes in the sport-specific section whom they had already discussed earlier. Furthermore, in some cases respondents tired toward the end of the interview and may not have named as many athletes in the sport-specific section as they might have if it had come earlier.

Pilot study results indicated that youngsters named two types of praiseworthy people: publicly known, famous people whom they had learned about primarily through the mass media, and personally known friends and family members whom they learned about primarily through face-to-face interaction. Therefore the general section and the sport-specific section of the interview each contained questions about both famous people and personal acquaintances.

Also, some youths in the pilot study said that they did not have any heroes but that they looked up to or admired certain people. To be certain of getting information from each respondent, and also to address the debate about the continued existence of heroes, each section of the interview was further subdivided into discussions of admirable people and heroes. As a prelude to their initial discussion in the beginning of the interview about admirable public figures, respondents were asked merely to name famous people; we then asked them if they thought any or all of these people were admirable. They were next asked if they considered any or all of the people they admired to be heroes. This multistage procedure may have also helped to ensure that anyone identified as a hero was actually considered heroic by the respondent. The interviewers added extra commentary as appropriate in an attempt to assure the young people that declining to name admirable people and/or heroes was legitimate. Respondents who declined were asked to give their reasons.

Table A.1   Interview Outline

I.   Exemplars in General
    A.   Famous, Publicly Known People
        1. Listing
        2. Admirable People
        3. Heroes
    B.   Personal Acquaintances
        1. Admirable People
        2. Heroes
    C.   Combined Ranking Task
    D.   Specific Questions About Respondent's Greatest Exemplar

II. Exemplars in Sport
    A.   Famous, Publicly Known People
        1. Admirable People
        2. Heroes
    B.   Personal Acquaintances
        1. Admirable People
        2. Heroes

Between the general and sport-specific sections of the interview, several less open-ended questions were posed. Respondents were asked to rank together all of their heroes (or people they considered admirable if they had no heroes)— both public figures and personal acquaintances. They were also asked several specific questions about the person they would most like to be like, and their greatest hero (or admirable person if they had no hero).

Respondents selected praiseworthy people by name and were permitted to identify as many as they wished. In most studies respondents have been limited in the number of people they could name; we thought that knowing the full array of people held in high regard might add insight. The youths were not provided with a list of specific people to choose from, but the interviewer mentioned a variety of types of people that might fit into the current category being discussed (i.e., for public figures—television stars or the characters they play, movie stars or the characters they play, comic or cartoon characters, characters in books, sports stars, music stars, church leaders, political or government leaders, military leaders; for personal acquaintances—family members, school teachers or leaders, friends, church ministers or leaders, Girl or Boy Scout leaders, recreation or playground leaders, coaches).

After the praiseworthy people were named, each respondent was asked to discuss why she or he held these people in high esteem. The goal here was to learn about the ways in which the respondents themselves characterized these people. We assumed that respondents could articulate the laudable qualities of the people they identified. They were not given abstract definitions of admirable people or heroes. Instead our objective was to obtain their own definitions of these people based on the characteristics they used to describe them. Some respondents provided considerable detail about these characteristics, others were relatively brief, and some were extremely reticent. Some youngsters talked about the praiseworthy qualities of every person they named, whereas others chose to consider only a few of those they listed. As might be expected, the 3rd graders had the most difficulty with this part of the interview, although extra time was spent in an effort to make them understand.

The principal investigator read the transcriptions to decide the ways the analyses would be structured and then to develop a coding system. Three major characteristics of praiseworthy people emerged, comprised of several subcategories: personal competence (expertise, endurance of hardships); social supportiveness (helpfulness, pleasant personality, sense of humor); and celebrity shallowness (fame, association with valued phenomena, and physical appearance). Two additional categories were negative characteristics and miscellaneous characteristics. Using this system, the principal investigator coded the youths' characterizations of the people they considered admirable and/or heroic.

Four major categories of public figures were also identified by the principal investigator: athletes, entertainers, political or military leaders, and others. Personal acquaintances were not categorized further because of their relatively small numbers.

Data analyses were carried out separately for admirable people and heroes. Quantitative data consisted of selection frequencies and frequencies with which particular characteristics were used to describe the people chosen. Analyses consisted of determining various percentages relevant to the overall concerns of the study. No inferential statistics were computed because there were variations across respondents regarding their total contributions to the data, and these were assumed to be unsystematic. These unsystematic variations resulted because respondents named different numbers of praiseworthy people and used various amounts and combinations of praiseworthy attributes to describe the people they chose.

Qualitative analyses were carried out by the principal investigator on respondents' characterizations of the two most frequently mentioned athletes, entertainers, and political or military leaders. In addition, a qualitative examination of reasons for declining to name heroes was conducted.

Several recommendations concerning methodological improvements can be made for future work of this nature. If the debate about the continued existence of athletic heroes remains of central interest, then data should pertain to heroes alone. There is little need to gather information about "merely admirable" people. This more narrow focus would permit greater depth and detail concerning respondents' hero characterizations. A relatively small sample (perhaps no more than 20) should be interviewed at great length with frequent probes for additional details. More limited information should also be obtained from a larger sample using a survey technique. Based on the mean number of heroes named by respondents in previous investigations, including the Greensboro study, respondents should be limited to identifying and discussing four to six general heroes, and four to six athletic heroes. They should be encouraged to discuss both personal acquaintances and public figures, and it should be made as legitimate as possible either to name heroes or to decline naming them.

Children and adolescents are not reliable in ranking their heroes according to importance. They show considerable variation when asked to do this several times during an interview. If rankings are needed, respondents could be asked to develop an initial rank-order one day and then asked to look at the order again later to make changes and confirm. It is also not particularly useful to ask respondents to compare and contrast heroes, or to group them according to similarities and differences. The time could be better spent probing for more details about characterizations of the individual people named. In addition, youths are rather uncomfortable with questions asking for their greatest hero or the person they would most prefer to be like because many respondents do not want to be like any one particular person. Rather, they usually list several individuals. Thus interview questions of this nature may not yield useful results (depending on what is being studied, of course). Finally, if young children are included among respondents, considerable attention should be given to developing specialized questions focused at their level of understanding.

Appendix B

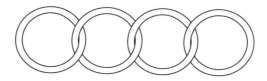

Greensboro Study: Interview Schedule

Part I. Introductory Comments

I. *Introduction*

A. I am working as an interviewer in a research project based at UNC-Greensboro, and the goal of my project is to find out more about the kinds of people or characters kids [students, people] your age look up to or admire.

B. We are interested in finding out more about this because it will help us to know more about the kinds of characteristics that are thought important for people to have in our society.

II. *Preliminary Comments*

A. We have already gotten your parents' permission for you to talk to me about this. I want to make sure that I also have your consent to participate and to tape-record our conversation.

B. Your comments will not ever be tied specifically to your name in any reports—we may use some of the things you say as examples in reporting the results of this study, but we will not tie your name specifically to your comments.

C. This is not a test—I know that at school you usually have tests where there are right and wrong answers, but there are no right or wrong answers to the questions I will be asking you. I am interested in your opinions or views about people you look up to or admire, and the questions are designed to help me learn about how you view these kinds of people or characters.

D. Try to use ordinary language—the language that you would use in talking with other kids your age. Sometimes when a tape recorder is on, people think that they have to use fancy language, or to say different kinds of things. Just try to talk as you ordinarily would in your everyday conversations with kids you know.

E. I may repeat some questions later in our discussion. This is because I want to make sure that I understand what you are saying to me. It is not meant to trick you in any way. I merely repeat things to make sure I am understanding clearly what it is you are telling me.

F. If at any point you wish to stop talking with me, let me know and we will end our conversation.

G. Do I have your permission to go ahead and ask you some questions about people you look up to or admire?

H. I will be making a few notes as we go along, and these are just so I can remember some of the things you say during our conversation.

Part II. Famous, Important People—General

I. *Famous, Important, Stand Out From the Crowd*

A. I want to start today by talking about people who are famous, important, or who stand out from the crowd.

B. Some examples of these kinds of people/characters are

television stars or the characters they play,

movie stars or the characters they play,

comic/cartoon characters,

characters in books,

sports stars,

music stars,

church leaders,

political/government leaders, and

military leaders (army/navy/air force/marines).

C. Think about some of the people/characters you or kids [students, people] your age think are famous, and tell me what it takes to make these people famous.

How do you view famous people or characters?

[Have them name famous people/characters, and then discuss what makes each of these famous.]

II. *Admire, Respect, Look Up To*

A. Are there some people/characters you or kids [students, people] your age really admire, respect, or look up to a lot?

Which ones?

What does it take for a famous person/character to be respected, admired or looked up to?

[Have them name the people/characters they admire and discuss why they admire, respect, or look up to them.]

What are the major similarities among these people/characters?

B. Are there some differences that you [kids, students, people] see among these famous people/characters who are admired a lot?

Describe the differences *or* distinguish among the types.

[Ask if the subject wants to group the famous people/characters who are admired a lot into a few groups and then describe how the groups differ.]

C. Of the famous people/characters we have just discussed, which ones do you or kids [students, people] you know admire or look up to the most?

Can you rank them from most admired to least admired?

What makes some of them more admirable than others?

III. *Heroes*

A. Of these famous people/characters who are admired or looked up to by you or by other kids [students, people] would you or kids [students, people] your age consider any or all of them heroes?

Which ones? *or* Why aren't any of them heroes?

What does it take for a famous person who is admired to be considered a hero?

[Have them name the people/characters they consider heroes and discuss why they consider them heroes.]

In your opinion, what makes a hero a hero?

What are the major similarities among these people/characters?

B. Are there some differences that you [kids, students, people] see among these people/characters who are heroes?

Describe the differences *or* distinguish among the types.

[Ask if the subject wants to group the heroes into a few groups and then describe how the groups differ.]

C. Of the heroes we have discussed, which ones do you or kids [students, people] you know think are the greatest or most important?

Can you rank them from greatest to least great?

What makes some of them greater than others?

Part III. Nonfamous People—General

I. *Nonfamous*

A. I want to continue by talking about some nonfamous people you may also admire or look up to.

B. Some examples of these kinds of people are

family members,

schoolteachers or leaders,

friends,

your church ministers or leaders,

Girl/Boy Scout leaders,
recreation/playground leaders,
coaches you have had, and
other nonfamous people who are admirable to you.

II. *Admire, Respect, Look Up To*
   A. Are there some of these nonfamous people you really admire, respect, or look up to a lot?

   Which ones?

   What about them do you particularly admire, respect, or look up to?

   [Have them name the people they admire and discuss why they admire, respect, or look up to them.]

   What are the major similarities among these people?

   B. Are there some differences that you see among these nonfamous people whom you admire a lot?

   Describe the differences *or* distinguish among the types.

   [Ask if the subject wants to group the people who are admired a lot into a few groups and then describe how the groups differ.]

   C. Of the nonfamous people we have just discussed, which ones do you admire or look up to the most?

   Can you rank them from most admired to least admired?

   What makes some of them more admirable than others?

III. *Heroes*
   A. Of these people who are nonfamous whom you admire or look up to, would you consider any or all of them heroes?

   Which ones? *or* Why aren't any of them heroes?

   What makes these people heroes to you?

   [Have them name the people they consider heroes and discuss why they consider them heroes.]

   In your opinion, what makes a hero a hero?

   What are the major similarities among these people?

   B. Are there some differences that you see among these nonfamous people who are heroes?

   Describe the differences *or* distinguish among the types.

   [Ask if the subject wants to group the heroes into a few groups and then describe how the groups differ.]

   C. Of these nonfamous heroes we have discussed, which ones do you think are the greatest or most important?

   Can you rank them from greatest to least great?

What makes some of them greater than others?

Part IV. Heroes—Directed Questions

To the Interviewer:

1. If the subject has indicated that he or she has one or more heroes, then use the word *hero* in this part of the interview. If the subject does not have heroes, then use the synonymous terms of people he or she *admires, respects,* or *looks up to.*
2. The word *hero* is used alone below; you must substitute the other phrases when necessary.

I. [Review the subject's heroes included under the famous and nonfamous sections.]

I would like you to try to rank all of these people now in one long list, starting with the greatest or most important hero and going on down to the least great. Which one do you think is most important to you? Which one is next most important? (Etc.)

II. Could you aspire to be just like your greatest hero? Or does he or she have qualities that most people can never attain?

Is there any one person that you would like to be just like?

If you had to choose one person to be like, who would it be? Why?

III. Is your greatest hero involved in violence? In what ways? Do you admire/condone/accept/approve of the violent actions of your hero?

IV. Is your greatest hero godlike? In what ways yes? In what ways no?

V. What couldn't you stand to see your greatest hero doing?

Who would you least want to see your greatest hero associate with? Why?

Who is the most unheroic person you can think of? What makes him or her so unheroic?

Part V. Famous, Important People—Sports

Now I would like to narrow our discussion to focus for awhile here at the end of the interview on sports stars.

I. *Admire, Respect, Look Up To*

A. Are there some famous sports stars you or kids [students, people] your age really admire, respect, or look up to a lot?

Which ones?

What does it take for a famous sports star to be admired, respected, or looked up to?

[Have them name the famous sports stars they admire and discuss why they admire, respect, or look up to them.]

Is their sports ability the most important thing that you admire?

What are the major similarities among these people?

B. Are there some differences that you [kids, students, people] see among these sports stars who are admired a lot?

Describe the differences *or* distinguish among the types.

[Ask if the subject wants to group sports stars who are admired a lot into a few groups and then describe how the groups differ.]

C. Of the famous sports stars we have just discussed, which ones do you or kids [students, people] you know admire or look up to the most?

Can you rank them from most admired to least admired?

What makes some of them more admirable than others?

II. *Heroes*

A. Of these famous sports stars who are admired or looked up to by you or by other kids [students, people], would you or other kids [students, people] your age consider any or all of them heroes?

Which ones? *or* Why aren't any of them heroes?

What does it take for a famous sports star who is admired to be considered as a hero?

[Have them name the famous sports stars they consider heroes and discuss why they consider them heroes.]

What are the major similarities among these people?

B. Are there some differences that you [kids, students, people] see among these sports stars who are heroes?

Describe the differences *or* distinguish among the types.

[Ask if the subject wants to group the sports heroes into a few groups and then describe how the groups differ.]

C. Of the sports heroes we have discussed, which ones do you or kids [students, people] you know think are the greatest or most important?

Can you rank them from greatest to least great?

What makes some of them greater than others?

III. *Comparisons With Other Heroic or Admired Famous People*

To Interviewer: If the subject has heroes, use the word *hero* here. If not, then use *admire, respect, look up to.*

What do you see as the main differences between famous sports heroes and other famous heroes who are not involved in sports?

What are the main similarities?

Part VI. Nonfamous People—Sports

Now I would like to end our discussion by talking about nonfamous people you admire, respect, or look up to whom you consider outstanding athletes—very good in sports.

Remember the kinds of nonfamous people we were talking about before included
family members,
schoolteachers or leaders,
friends,
your church ministers or leaders,
Girl/Boy Scout leaders,
recreation/playground leaders,
coaches you have had, and
other nonfamous people who are admirable to you.

I.   *Admire, Respect, Look Up To*

A. Are there some nonfamous people who are outstanding athletes or very good in sports you really admire, respect, or look up to a lot?

Which ones?

What about them do you particularly admire, respect or look up to?

[Have them name the people they admire and discuss why they admire, respect, or look up to them.]

Is their sports ability the most important thing that you admire?

What are the major similarities among these people?

B. Are there some differences that you see among these nonfamous people who are good in sports whom you admire a lot?

Describe the differences *or* distinguish among the types.

[Ask if the subject wants to group the people who are admired a lot into a few groups and then describe how the groups differ.]

C. Of the nonfamous people who are good in sports we have just discussed, which ones do you admire or look up to the most?

Can you rank them from most admired to least admired?

What makes some of them more admirable than others?

II. *Heroes*

A. Of these people who are nonfamous and good in sports whom you admire or look up to, would you consider any or all of them heroes?

Which ones? *or* Why aren't any of them heroes?

What makes these people heroes to you?

[Have them name the people they consider heroes and discuss why they consider them heroes.]

What are the major similarities among these people?

B. Are there some differences that you see among these nonfamous people who are good in sports whom you consider heroes?

Describe the differences *or* distinguish among the types.

[Ask if the subject wants to group the heroes into a few groups and then describe how the groups differ.]

C. Of these nonfamous heroes we have discussed who are good in sports, which ones do you think are the greatest or most important?

Can you rank them from greatest to least great?

What makes some of them greater than others?

III. *Comparisons With Other Heroic/Admired Nonfamous People*

To Interviewer: If the subject has heroes use the word *hero* here. If not, then use *admire, respect, look up to.*

What do you see as the main differences between nonfamous sports heroes and other nonfamous heroes who are not involved in sports?

What are the main similarities?

Thank you very much for helping me with this project.

References

Among Wisconsin students, mom and dad are no. 1. (1985, July 3). *The Chronicle of Higher Education*, **30**(18), p. 2.

Anderson, D.F. (1979). Sport spectatorship: Appropriation of an identity or appraisal of self. *Review of Sport and Leisure*, **4**(2), 115-127.

Averill, L.A. (1950, July 22). The impact of a changing culture upon pubescent ideals. *School and Society*, 49-53.

Axthelm, P. (1979, August 6). Where have all the heroes gone? *Newsweek*, pp. 44-50.

Balswick, J., & Ingoldsby, B. (1982). Heroes and heroines among American adolescents. *Sex Roles*, **8**, 243-249.

Bandura, A. (1969). Social-learning theory of identificatory processes. In D.A. Goslin (Ed.), *Handbook of socialization theory and research* (pp. 213-262). Chicago: Rand McNally.

Bandura, A. (1971a). Analysis of modeling processes. In A. Bandura (Ed.), *Psychological modeling: Conflicting theories* (pp. 1-62). Chicago: Aldine/Atherton.

Bandura, A. (1971b). *Social learning theory*. Morristown, NJ: General Learning.

Barney, R.K., & Barney, D.E. (1989, May). *Night of heroes: Flags, flowers, and last hurrahs*. Paper presented at the meeting of the North American Society for Sport History, Clemson, SC.

Bennett, W.J. (1977, August 15). Let's bring back heroes. *Newsweek*, p. 3.

Birrell, S. (1981). Sport as ritual: Interpretations from Durkheim to Goffman. *Social Forces*, **60**, 354-376.

Bloom, J.D. (1988). Joe Namath and Super Bowl III: An interpretation of style. *Journal of Sport History*, **15**(1), 64-74.

Boorstin, D.J. (1980). *The image: A guide to pseudo-events in America*. New York: Atheneum. (Original work published 1961)

Bredemeier, B.J., Weiss, M.R., Shields, D.L., & Cooper, B.A.B. (1986). The relationship of sport involvement with children's moral reasoning and aggression tendencies. *Journal of Sport Psychology*, **8**, 304-318.

Browne, R.B. (1983). Hero with 2000 faces. In R.B. Browne & M.W. Fishwick (Eds.), *The hero in transition* (pp. 91-106). Bowling Green, OH: Bowling Green University Popular Press.

Bryant, J. (1989). Viewers' enjoyment of televised sports violence. In L.A. Wenner (Ed.), *Media, sports, and society* (pp. 270-289). Newbury Park, CA: Sage.

Campbell, J. (1968). *The hero with a thousand faces* (2nd ed.). Princeton, NJ: Princeton University Press.

Castine, S.C., & Roberts, G.C. (1974). Modeling in the socialization process of the black athlete. *International Review of Sport Sociology*, **9**(3-4), 59-74.

Caughey, J.L. (1984). *Imaginary social worlds: A cultural approach.* Lincoln, NE: University of Nebraska Press.

Chalip, P., & Chalip, L. (1989). Olympic athletes as American heroes. In R. Jackson (Ed.), *The Olympic movement and the mass media: Past, present and future issues* (pp. 11/3-11/26). Calgary: Hurford Enterprises.

Coakley, J.J. (1986). *Sport in society: Issues and controversies* (3rd ed.). St. Louis: Times Mirror/Mosby.

Coakley, J.J. (1990). *Sport in society: Issues and controversies* (4th ed.). St. Louis: Times Mirror/Mosby.

Condit, C.M. (1989). The rhetorical limits of polysemy. *Critical Studies in Mass Communication,* **6**(2), 103-122.

Cooper, D., Livingood, A.B., & Kurz, R.B. (1981). Children's choice of sports heroes and heroines: The role of child-hero similarity. *Psychological Documents,* **11**(4), 85. (Ms. No. 2376)

Crepeau, R.C. (1981). Sport, heroes and myth. *Journal of Sport and Social Issues,* **5**, 23-31.

Crepeau, R.C. (1985). Where have you gone, Frank Merriwell? The decline of the American sports hero. In W.L. Umphlett (Ed.), *American sport culture: The humanistic dimensions* (pp. 76-82). Cranbury, NJ: Associated University Presses.

Csikszentmihalyi, M., & Lyons, B. (1982). *The selection of behavioral traits: Reasons for admiring people.* Unpublished manuscript, University of Chicago.

Cummings, R. (1972). The Superbowl society. In R.B. Browne, M. Fishwick, & M.T. Mardsen (Eds.), *Heroes of popular culture* (pp. 101-111). Bowling Green, OH: Bowling Green University Popular Press.

Decision Research Corporation. (1984). *Summary of research with teenagers.* Lexington, MA: Author.

Deford, F. (1969, June 9). What price heroes? *Sports Illustrated,* pp. 32-34, 37, 40.

Donnelly, P., Hargreaves, J., & Tomlinson, A. (Eds.) (1992). British cultural studies and sport [Special issue]. *Sociology of Sport Journal,* **9**(2).

Duncan, M.C., & Brummett, B. (1987). The mediation of spectator sport. *Research Quarterly for Exercise and Sport,* **58**, 168-177.

Eitzen, D.S., & Sage, G.H. (1991). *Sociology of American sport* (5th ed.). Madison, WI: Brown & Benchmark.

Elkind, D. (1981). *The hurried child: Growing up too fast too soon.* Reading, MA: Addison-Wesley.

Eskenazi, G. (1982, October 31). The changing face of sports in America. *The Winston-Salem Journal,* p. D11.

Fairlie, H. (1978, November). Too rich for heroes. *Harper's,* pp. 33-37, 40, 42-43, 97-98.

Fishwick, M.W. (1983). The hero in transition: Introduction. In R.B. Browne & M.W. Fishwick (Eds.), *The hero in transition,* pp. 5-13. Bowling Green, OH: Bowling Green University Popular Press.

Fiske, J. (1987). *Television culture.* London: Routledge.

Fortino, D. (1984, November). Why kids need heroes. *Parents*, pp. 214, 218, 221-222, 225-226, 229.

Frieze, I.H., Parsons, J.E., Johnson, P.B., Ruble, D.N., & Zellman, G.L. (1978). *Women and sex roles: A social psychological perspective*. New York: W.W. Norton.

Gamarnikow, E., Morgan, D.H.J., Purvis, J., & Taylorson, D. (1983). *The public and the private*. London: Heinemann.

Gamson, J. (1992). The assembly line of greatness: Celebrity in twentieth-century America. *Critical Studies in Mass Communication*, **9**, 1-24.

Gerzon, M. (1982). *A choice of heroes: The changing faces of American manhood*. Boston: Houghton Mifflin.

Gilbert, B. (1972, December 25). Gleanings from a troubled time. *Sports Illustrated*, pp. 34-38, 43-46.

Goffman, E. (1967). *Interaction ritual: Essays on face-to-face behavior*. Garden City, NY: Anchor Books.

Goode, W.J. (1978). *The celebration of heroes: Prestige as a social control system*. Berkeley: University of California Press.

Gould, S.J. (1986, August). Entropic homogeneity isn't why no one hits .400 any more. *Discover*, pp. 60-66.

Greenberg, B.S., Simmons, K.W., Hogan, L., & Atkin, C. (1980). Three seasons of television characters: A demographic analysis. *Journal of Broadcasting*, **24**, 49-60.

Greene, T.P. (1970). *America's heroes: The changing models of success in American magazines*. New York: Oxford University Press.

Greenstein, F.I. (1969). *Children and politics* (rev. ed.). New Haven, CT: Yale University Press.

Gurko, L. (1953). *Heroes, highbrows and the popular mind*. Indianapolis: Bobbs-Merrill.

Harris, J.C., & Hills, L.A. (1993). Telling the story: Narrative in newspaper accounts of a men's collegiate basketball tournament. *Research Quarterly for Exercise and Sport*, **64**, 108-121.

Heroes of young America: A national poll. (1980). In H.U. Lane (Ed.), *The world almanac and book of facts 1981* (p. 273). New York: Newspaper Enterprise Association.

Heroes of young America: The second annual poll. (1981). In H.U. Lane (Ed.), *The world almanac and book of facts 1982* (p. 39). New York: Newspaper Enterprise Association.

Heroes of young America: The sixth annual poll. (1985). In H.U. Lane (Ed.), *The world almanac and book of facts 1986* (p. 38). New York: Newspaper Enterprise Association.

Heroes of young America: The seventh annual poll. (1986). In M.S. Hoffman (Ed.), *The world almanac and book of facts 1987* (p. 34). New York: Pharos.

Heroes of young America: The eighth annual poll. (1987). In M.S. Hoffman (Ed.), *The world almanac and book of facts 1988* (p. 34). New York: Pharos.

Heroes of young America: The ninth annual poll. (1988). In M.S. Hoffman (Ed.), *The world almanac and book of facts 1989* (p. 33). New York: Pharos.

Heroes of young America: The tenth annual poll. (1989). In M.S. Hoffman (Ed.), *The world almanac and book of facts 1990* (pp. 32-33). New York: Pharos.

Heroes of young America: The eleventh annual poll. (1990). In M.S. Hoffman (Ed.), *The world almanac and book of facts 1991* (pp. 32-33). New York: Pharos.

Heroes of young America: The twelfth annual poll. (1991). In M.S. Hoffman (Ed.), *The world almanac and book of facts 1992* (p. 32). New York: Pharos.

Higgs, R.J. (1981). *Laurel & thorn: The athlete in American literature.* Lexington, KY: University Press of Kentucky.

Hilliard, D.C. (1984). Media images of male and female professional athletes: An interpretive analysis of magazine articles. *Sociology of Sport Journal,* **1**(3), 251-262.

Hills, L.A. (1992). *Mass media portrayals of drug use in sports.* Unpublished master's thesis, University of North Carolina at Greensboro.

Hughes, R., & Coakley, J. (1984). Mass society and the commercialization of sport. *Sociology of Sport Journal,* **1**, 57-63.

Hoberman, J.M. (1992). *Mortal engines: The science of performance and the dehumanization of sport.* New York: Free Press.

Huston, A.C. (1983). Sex-typing. In P.H. Mussen (Ed.), *Handbook of child psychology: Vol. 4. Socialization, personality, and social development* (pp. 387-467). New York: John Wiley.

Hyman, H.H. (1975). Reference individuals and reference idols. In L.A. Coser (Ed.), *The idea of social structure: Papers in honor of Robert K. Merton* (pp. 265-282). New York: Harcourt Brace Jovanovich.

Hyman, H.H., & Singer, E. (Eds.) (1968). *Readings in reference group theory and research.* New York: Free Press.

Ingham, A.G., Howell, J.W., & Schilperoot, T.S. (1987). Professional sports and community: A review and exegesis. In K.B. Pandolf (Ed.), *Exercise and Sport Sciences Reviews,* **15**, 427-465.

Ingham, A.G., Howell, J.W., & Swetman, R.D. (1993). Evaluating sport "hero/ines": Contents, forms, and social relations. *Quest,* **45**, 197-210.

Ingham, A.G., Loy, J.W., & Swetman, R.D. (1979). Sport, heroes, and society: Issues of transformation and reproduction. *Working Papers in the Sociological Study of Sports and Leisure,* **2**(4). Kingston, Ontario: Sports Studies Research Group, School of Physical and Health Education, Queen's University.

Isaacs, N.D. (1978). *Jock culture U.S.A.* New York: W.W. Norton.

Janes, B.T. (1982). American heroes. *Et Cetera,* **39**(2), 180-183.

Johnson, A.T. (1985). The sports franchise relocation issue and public policy responses. In A.T. Johnson & J.H. Frey (Eds.), *Government and sport: The public policy issues* (pp. 219-247). Totowa, NJ: Rowman & Allanheld.

Johnson, W.O. (1983, August 15). What's happened to our heroes? *Sports Illustrated,* pp. 32-34, 38, 40, 42.

Kahn, J.J. (1979). The hero world of the adolescent male: A descriptive/Jungian perspective. (Doctoral dissertation, California School of Professional Psychology, 1978). *Dissertation Abstracts International*, **39**, 3520B-3521B.

Kahn, R. (1974, October). Where have all our heroes gone? *Esquire*, pp. 141-143, 387-389.

Kennedy, R., & Williamson, N. (1978, July 31). The fans: Are they up in arms? *Sports Illustrated*, pp. 34-42, 47, 49-50.

Kinkema, K.M., & Harris, J.C. (1992). Sport and the mass media. *Exercise and Sport Sciences Reviews*, **20**, 127-159.

Klapp, O.E. (1956). American villain-types. *American Sociological Review*, **21**, 337-340.

Klapp, O.E. (1962). *Heroes, villains, and fools: The changing American character*. Englewood Cliffs, NJ: Prentice-Hall.

Klapp, O.E. (1969). *Collective search for identity*. New York: Holt, Rinehart and Winston.

Laponce, J.A. (1986). Heroes and villains: Locating politics between the positive and the negative. *Social Science Information*, **25**(2), 421-437.

Lever, J. (1976). Sex differences in the games children play. *Social Problems*, **23**, 478-487.

Lewis, K. (1985). Superstardom and transcendence. *Arete: The Journal of Sport Literature*, **2**(2), 47-54.

Lewis, L.S. (1965). Political heroes: 1936 and 1960. *Journalism Quarterly*, **42**, 116-118.

Lipsky, R. (1981). *How we play the game: Why sports dominate American life*. Boston: Beacon Press.

Lipsyte, R. (1975). *SportsWorld: An American dreamland*. New York: Quadrangle Books.

Lowenthal, L. (1956). Biographies in popular magazines. In W. Petersen (Ed.), *American social patterns: Studies of race relations, popular heroes, voting, union democracy, and government bureaucracy* (pp. 63-118). Garden City, NY: Doubleday Anchor. (Original work published 1944)

Loy, J.W., & Hesketh, G.L. (1984). The agon motif: A prolegomenon for the study of agonetic behavior. In K. Olin (Ed.), *Contribution of sociology to the study of sport* (pp. 31-50). Jyvaskyla, Finland: University of Jyvaskyla Press.

Lubin, H. (Ed.) (1968). *Heroes and anti-heroes: A reader in depth*. San Francisco: Chandler.

MacAloon, J.J. (1984a). Introduction: Cultural performances, culture theory. In J.J. MacAloon (Ed.), *Rite, drama, festival, spectacle: Rehearsals toward a theory of cultural performance* (pp. 1-15). Philadelphia: Institute for the Study of Human Issues.

MacAloon, J.J. (1984b). Olympic Games and the theory of spectacle in modern societies. In J.J. MacAloon (Ed.), *Rite, drama, festival, spectacle: Rehearsals toward a theory of cultural performance* (pp. 241-280). Philadelphia: Institute for the Study of Human Issues.

MacAloon, J.J. (1987). An observer's view of sport sociology. *Sociology of Sport Journal*, **4**, 103-115.

MacAloon, J.J. (1990). Steroids and the state: Dubin, melodrama and the accomplishment of innocence. *Public Culture*, **2**(2), 41-64.

Manning, F.E. (1983). Cosmos and chaos: Celebration in the modern world. In F.E. Manning (Ed.), *The celebration of society: Perspectives on contemporary cultural performance* (pp. 3-30). Bowling Green, OH: Bowling Green University Popular Press.

Marovelli, E., & Crawford, S.A.G.M. (1987). Mass media influence on female high school athletes' identification with professional athletes. *International Journal of Sport Psychology*, **18**(3), 231-236.

McBee, S. (1985, April 22). Heroes are back: Young Americans tell why. *U.S. News and World Report*, pp. 44-48.

McCormack, J.B. (1984). *Interpersonal influences and the channeling of goals in adolescence*. Unpublished doctoral dissertation, University of Chicago.

McEvoy, A., & Erickson, E.L. (1981). Heroes and villains: A conceptual strategy for assessing their influence. *Sociological Focus*, **14**(2), 111-122.

McNulty, T.J. (1986, January 25). So many heroes so few heroic deeds. *San Jose Mercury News*, pp. 1C, 15C.

Messenger, C.K. (1981). *Sport and the spirit of play in American fiction: Hawthorne to Faulkner*. New York: Columbia University Press.

Meyrowitz, J. (1984, July). Politics in the video eye: Where have all the heroes gone? *Psychology Today*, pp. 46-51.

Miller Brewing Company. (1983). *The Miller Lite report on American attitudes toward sports*. Milwaukee: Author.

Miller, M.S. (1976, August). Who are the kids' heroes and heroines? *Ladies Home Journal*, pp. 108-109.

Morford, W.R., & Clark, S.J. (1976). The agon motif. In J. Keogh & R.S. Hutton (Eds.), *Exercise and Sport Sciences Reviews*, **4**, 163-193. Santa Barbara, CA: Journal Publishing Affiliates.

Morse, M. (1983). Sport on television: Replay and display. In A.E. Kaplan (Ed.), *Regarding television: Critical approaches—an anthology* (pp. 44-66). Frederick, MD: University Publications of America and the American Film Institute.

Mueller, J.E. (1973). *War, presidents and public opinion*. New York: John Wiley.

Nixon, H.L., II. (1984). *Sport and the American dream*. New York: Leisure Press.

O'Brien, M. (1981). *The politics of reproduction*. London: Routledge & Kegan Paul.

On the difficulty of being a contemporary hero. (1966, June 24). *Time*, pp. 32-33.

Oriard, M.V. (1982). *Dreaming of heroes: American sports fiction, 1868-1980*. Chicago: Nelson-Hall.

Ortner, S.B., & Whitehead, H. (1981). Introduction: Accounting for sexual meanings. In S.B. Ortner & H. Whitehead (Eds.), *Sexual meanings: The cultural construction of gender and sexuality* (pp. 1-27). Cambridge, England: Cambridge University Press.

Palmer, M.D. (1973). The sports novel: Mythic heroes and natural men. *Quest*, **19**, 49-58.

Pretzinger, K. (1976). The American hero yesterday and today. *Humboldt Journal of Social Relations*, **4**, 36-40.

Rader, B.G. (1984). *In its own image: How television has transformed sports*. New York: Free Press.

Rein, I.J., Kotler, P., & Stoller, M.R. (1987). *High visibility*. New York: Dodd & Mead.

Reising, R.W. (1971). "Where have all our heroes gone?" Some insights into sports figures in modern American literature. *Quest*, **16**, 1-12.

Rollin, R.B. (Ed.) (1973). *Hero/anti-hero*. New York: McGraw-Hill.

Rollin, R.R. (1983). The Lone Ranger and Lenny Skutnik: The hero as popular culture. In R.B. Browne & M.W. Fishwick (Eds.), *The hero in transition* (pp. 14-45). Bowling Green, OH: Bowling Green University Popular Press.

Rosaldo, M.Z. (1974). Woman, culture, and society: A theoretical overview. In M.Z. Rosaldo & L. Lamphere (Eds.), *Woman, culture, and society* (pp. 17-42). Stanford, CA: Stanford University Press.

Rudman, W.J. (1986). The sport mystique in black culture. *Sociology of Sport Journal*, **3**, 305-319.

Russell, G.W. (1979). Hero selection by Canadian ice hockey players: Skill or aggression? *Canadian Journal of Applied Sport Sciences*, **4**, 309-313.

Russell, G.W., & Giurissevich, M.G. (1985, May). *The exemplars of adolescents: Their influence and quality*. Paper presented at the meeting of the Banff Annual Seminar in Cognitive Science, Banff, Alberta.

Schillaci, P. (1978, December). Where have all the heroes gone? *Media and Methods*, pp. 12-14, 16-18, 23-24.

Schimmel, K.S. (1987). *Professional sport franchise relocation within the context of urban politics: A case study*. Unpublished master's thesis, Miami University, Oxford, OH.

Schimmel, K.S., Ingham, A.G., & Howell, J.W. (1993). Professional team sport and the American city: Urban politics and franchise relocations. In A.G. Ingham & J.W. Loy (Eds.), *Sport in social development* (pp. 211-244). Champaign, IL: Human Kinetics.

Schlesinger, A.M., Jr. (1968). The decline of heroes. In H. Lubin (Ed.), *Heroes and anti-heroes: A reader in depth* (pp. 341-351). San Francisco: Chandler. (Original work published 1958)

Schmitt, R.L. (1972). *The reference other orientation: An extension of the reference group concept*. Carbondale, IL: Southern Illinois University Press.

Sirota, D. (1978). The electronic minstrel: Towards a new folklore and hero. *Et Cetera*, **35**(3), 302-309.

Skipper, J.K., Jr. (1984). The sociological significance of nicknames: The case of baseball players. *Journal of Sport Behavior*, **7**, 28-38.

Skipper, J.K., Jr. (1985). Nicknames, folk heroes, and assimilation: Black league baseball players, 1884-1950. *Journal of Sport Behavior*, **8**(2), 100-114.

Smelstor, M., & Billman, C. (1978). Ballyhoo and debunk: The unmaking of American political and sports heroes. *North Dakota Quarterly*, **46**(3), 4-11.

Smith, G. (1973). The sport hero: An endangered species. *Quest*, **19**, 59-70.

Smith, G.J. (1976). An examination of the phenomenon of sports hero worship. *Canadian Journal of Applied Sports Sciences*, **1**(4), 259-270.

Smith, T.W. (1986). The polls: The most admired man and woman. *Public Opinion Quarterly*, **50**, 573-583.

Spreitzer, E., & Snyder, E.E. (1990). Sports within the black subculture: A matter of social class or a distinctive subculture? *Journal of Sport and Social Issues*, **14**, 48-58.

The top ten. (1977, June 13). *Sports Illustrated*, p. 13.

U.S. Bureau of the Census (1984). *Statistical abstract of the United States: 1985*. Washington, DC: U.S. Government Printing Office.

U.S. Bureau of the Census (1992). *Statistical abstract of the United States: 1992*. Washington, DC: U.S. Government Printing Office.

Umphlett, W.L. (1975). *The sporting myth and the American experience: Studies in contemporary fiction*. Cranbury, NJ: Associated University Presses.

Vander Velden, L. (1986). Heroes and bad winners: Cultural differences. In L. Vander Velden & J.H. Humphrey (Eds.), *Psychology and sociology of sport: Current selected research: Vol. 1* (pp. 205-220). New York: AMS Press.

Voigt, D.Q. (1976). *America through baseball*. Chicago: Nelson-Hall.

Voigt, D.Q. (1978). Myths after baseball: Notes on myths in sports. *Quest*, **30**, 46-57.

Webb, M. (1974). Sunday heroes: The emergence of the professional football novel. *Journal of Popular Culture*, **8**(2), 452-461.

Wecter, D. (1941). *The hero in America: A chronicle of hero-worship*. New York: Charles Scribner's Sons.

Zimmerman, R. (1973). Children's heroes vis-a-vis textbook heroes. *Negro Educational Review*, **24**(3-4), 157-162.

Index

Political/military leaders as heroes
  characterizations of, 80-81, 90-92, 94, 107
  choice of
    age in, 56, 61, 109
    frequency of, 30, 31-32, 33, 34, 35
    gender in, 42-45
    race in, 51, 52, 53, 54, 55, 56
  and existence of heroes, 110
  specific leaders, 30, 31-32, 53, 90-92
Powell, Colin, 53
Pretzinger, K., 37
Prosocial characteristics, 67-68. *See also* Social supportiveness of heroes
Public image of athletes, 69, 70. *See also* Media coverage

Q
Quayle, Dan, 117

R
Race, influence of
  on characterizations
    of entertainers, 82, 94, 109
    of famous athletes, 78, 79, 81-84, 94
    overview of, 70, 74-75, 108-109
    of personally known athletes, 97-98
    previous research on, 70
  on choice of heroes, 41, 48-56, 61, 63, 108-109
  previous research on, 49, 55, 70
  recommendations for future research on, 116
Race, of professional athletes, 49, 51
Racial stereotyping (racism), influence of, 18, 54, 84, 115
Rader, B.G., 3, 13-14, 15, 21-22
Reagan, Ronald, 30, 31-32, 53, 90-92
Recording artists as heroes, 45, 53
Reinforcing heroes, 69
Reising, R.W., 18, 19, 20
Research design for Greensboro study. *See* Methodology for Greensboro study
Reynolds, Burt, 88-90
Robinson, Jackie, 67
Ross, Diana, 88-90
Russell, G.W., 71
Ruth, Babe, 67

S
Schillaci, P., 37
Screen Actors Guild, 45, 53
Seductive heroes, 69
Seles, Monica, 117
Self-concept, 11-12
Self-confidence, 70
Selfishness, 70, 74
Sense of humor, 73
Sexism, 18
Sexual attractiveness, 68
Shallowness of heroes
  in characterizations
    appearance in, 70, 73, 74, 77, 78, 89-90, 97